The study of the deliberate allusion by one author to the words of a previous author has long been central to Latin philology, which has developed some enviable critical tools for scrutinizing the subtleties of allusive art. However, literary Romanists have been diffident about situating such work within the more spacious inquiries into intertextuality now current – inquiries which find *all* discourse to be constituted by negotiations between texts, or between other cultural expressions analysable as 'texts'. This book represents a new attempt to find (or recover) some space for the study of allusion – as a project of continuing vitality – within an excitingly enlarged universe of intertexts. Its five chapters can be read either as self-contained essays or as a cumulative exploration of dynamics between poems, and among poets and readers, in Roman literary history. The issues addressed are of interest not just to classicists but also to students of later poetic traditions for which Roman practice was foundational. All Latin and Greek is translated or closely paraphrased.

ROMAN LITERATURE
AND ITS CONTEXTS

Allusion and intertext

ROMAN LITERATURE
AND ITS CONTEXTS

Series editors
Denis Feeney and Stephen Hinds

This series promotes approaches to Roman literature which are open to dialogue with current work in other areas of the classics, and in the humanities at large. The pursuit of contacts with cognate fields such as social history, anthropology, history of thought, linguistics and literary theory is in the best traditions of classical scholarship: the study of Roman literature, no less than Greek, has much to gain from engaging with these other contexts and intellectual traditions. The series offers a forum in which readers of Latin texts can sharpen their readings by placing them in broader and better-defined contexts, and in which other classicists and humanists can explore the general or particular implications of their work for readers of Latin texts. The books all constitute original and innovative research and are envisaged as suggestive essays whose aim is to stimulate debate.

Other books in the series

Allusion and intertext

Dynamics of appropriation in Roman poetry

Stephen Hinds

Professor of Classics,
University of Washington, Seattle

CAMBRIDGE
UNIVERSITY PRESS

PUBLISHED BY THE PRESS SYNDICATE OF THE UNIVERSITY OF CAMBRIDGE
The Pitt Building, Trumpington Street, Cambridge CB2 1RP, United Kingdom

CAMBRIDGE UNIVERSITY PRESS
The Edinburgh Building, Cambridge CB2 2RU, United Kingdom
40 West 20th Street, New York, NY 10011-4211, USA
10 Stamford Road, Oakleigh, Melbourne 3166, Australia

First published 1998

Printed in the United Kingdom at the University Press, Cambridge

Typeset in Times $9\frac{1}{2}$/12 pt

A catalogue record for this book is available from the British Library

Library of Congress cataloguing in publication data

Hinds, Stephen
Allusion and intertext: dynamics of appropriation in Roman poetry
/ Stephen Hinds
p. cm. (Roman literature and its contexts)
Includes bibliographical references and index.
ISBN 0 521 57186 3 (hardback) ISBN 0 521 57677 6 (paperback)
1. Latin poetry – History and criticism. 2. Influence (Literary,
artistic, etc.). 3. Repetition (Rhetoric). 4. Rome – In literature.
5. Rhetoric, Ancient. 6. Intertextuality. 7. Allusions.
I. Title. II. Series.
PA6047.H56 1998
871'.0109–dc21 98-6744
CIP

ISBN 0 521 57186 3 hardback
ISBN 0 521 57677 6 paperback

VN

For C.M.C.

Contents

Preface

Whenever we describe the world, consciously or unconsciously we measure our descriptions against previous descriptions of the world. The words which we use have always been used before; we never have a monopoly on their contexts and connotations. This book addresses an interest in texts and traditions in which this inevitability of intertextual relation is complicated by a high level of linguistic and literary self-awareness on the part of the individual language-user – in texts and traditions in which authors and readers, not content to be acted upon passively by tradition, seek to shape and define it to their own specifications.

In this last sentence, I have arrived by a circuitous route at what to literary Romanists has often seemed the *only* kind of intertext worth studying: that is, the deliberate allusion by one author to the words of a previous author. Isolating and identifying such 'allusions' has for at least the past century been the most characteristic project of Latin philology; and, in scrutinizing individual cases, we Romanists typically argue with a degree of focus and precision which critics in other fields should envy. However, we have tended to be more diffident in situating this tidy and circumscribed study within the more spacious inquiries into intertextuality dominant in much later twentieth-century work – inquiries which find *all* discourse to be constituted by negotiations between texts, or between other cultural expressions analysable as 'texts'. We are by now no strangers to such modes of inquiry; but, whether attracted or repelled by them, most of us have not yet quite decided how (or if) to reconcile them with our old institutional ways.

The following five chapters represent a new attempt to find (or re-

cover) some space for the study of allusion – as a project of continuing
vitality – within an excitingly enlarged universe of intertexts. This critical
theoretical enterprise is undertaken in the context and cause of a sus-
tained exploration of dynamics between poems, and among poets and
readers, in Roman literary history. A book of some 145 pages must aim
to be suggestive rather than comprehensive, and in choosing my case-
studies I have favoured certain areas: epic and elegy, works at the edge of
the modern academic canon, Statius' *Achilleid* as well as Virgil and Ovid.
Every chapter can be read as a self-contained essay; but the essays are
designed to be complementary and cumulative, each drawing something
from ideas and procedures developed in the course of its predecessors.

I hope that this book will strike most readers as a pluralist one in its
critical emphases – which is not to say that it seeks to be somehow
neutral or post-theoretical. Some critical metaphors for the intertextual
relation privilege the agency of the author, some that of the reader, some
that of the text itself; some describe a later text as acting upon an earlier
one, some an earlier text as acting upon a later one, some an action
which is reciprocal ('Y alludes to X', 'X influences Y', 'X and Y are in
dialogue'); certain terms embrace intentionality, others deny or occlude
it (e.g. 'intertextuality' itself). It is thus impossible to adopt a wholly
neutral position or to find wholly neutral terms in embarking upon an
inquiry such as this; and the conscientious critic will resist the impulse to
naturalize his or her own terminological choices in such a way as to
preempt debate upon them.

My book owes much to Pauline Hire of Cambridge University Press,
and to the example of the pioneering authors who have established such
a distinctive idiom for this young series. Three of those authors, Philip
Hardie, Duncan Kennedy and Charles Martindale, also offered substan-
tive comments on major drafts, as did Alessandro Barchiesi, Netta
Berlin, Peter Bing, Jim Clauss, Ellen Finkelpearl, Simon Goldhill,
Michael Halleran, John Henderson, Alison Keith, Jim O'Hara, Jim
Porter, Patricia Rosenmeyer and Stephen Thielke. I learned much from
audiences at Bristol, California (Berkeley), California (Los Angeles),
Harvard, Iowa, Keele, Leeds, Michigan, Ohio State, Oxford, Victoria,
Washington, Wesleyan and Wisconsin, and at meetings of the APA (San
Francisco), CAMWS (Austin), CAPN (Seattle and Banff), and the
Greek and Roman Societies (Cambridge Triennial). My colleagues, first
at Michigan and then at Washington, were generous in their intellectual

support, as also were students in graduate classes on History of Roman Literature (Michigan), Ovid's *Metamorphoses* and Statius (Washington), with whom some of these ideas were first discussed. At the Press I found in Muriel Hall a vigilant and sensitive copy-editor. The place of honour in my acknowledgements goes to two friends who read and reread successive drafts of this book, improving it each time in countless ways, large and small: Denis Feeney, my co-editor, and Catherine Connors, my colleague and wife.

It is a pleasure to thank the National Endowment for the Humanities for the award in 1994–5 of a Fellowship for University Teachers, the University of Washington for a period of sabbatical leave, and the University of Washington Graduate School and Department of Classics for sponsorship of travel. An earlier version of chapter 1, sections 1 and 2, appeared in *Hermathena* 158 (1995), 41–51; a version of chapter 5 will appear soon in a collection of essays in *Materiali e Discussioni*.

Abbreviations

CHCL *The Cambridge History of Classical Literature*. Cambridge 1982–5

OED *The Oxford English Dictionary*. 2nd ed. Oxford 1989

OLD *The Oxford Latin Dictionary*. Oxford 1968–82

SH H. Lloyd-Jones and P. Parsons, *Supplementum Hellenisticum*. Berlin and New York 1983

TLL *Thesaurus Linguae Latinae*. Leipzig 1900–

CHAPTER

I

Reflexivity: allusion and self-annotation

We should notice when the subject-matter of an allusion is at one with the impulse that underlies the making of allusions at all, because it is characteristic of art to find energy and delight in an enacting of that which it is saying, and to be rendered vigilant by a consciousness of metaphors and analogies which relate its literary practices to the great world.

(Christopher Ricks, 'Allusion: the poet as heir', 209)

Bitter constraint, and sad occasion dear
(Milton, *Lycidas* 6)

. . . sweet enforcement and remembrance dear
(Keats, *Ode to Psyche* 2)[1]

1 Incorporating the Alexandrian footnote

One may usefully identify a mannerism, by no means peculiar to Roman literature but especially well developed in Roman literature, whereby alluding poets exert themselves to draw attention to the fact that they are alluding, and to reflect upon the nature of their allusive activity. Certain allusions are so constructed as to carry a kind of built-in commentary, a kind of reflexive annotation, which underlines or intensifies their demand to be interpreted *as* allusions.

In its most basic form, the mannerism corresponds to the phenomenon which David Ross has labelled the 'Alexandrian footnote':[2] viz the

---

[1] I cite Keats's 'remembrance' of Milton after Hartman (1983), 217.
[2] Ross (1975), 78.

I

signalling of specific allusion by a poet through seemingly general appeals to tradition and report, such as 'the story goes' (*fama est*), 'they relate' (*ferunt*), or 'it is said' (*dicitur*). Consider, for example, the opening lines of Catullus 64, on the departure of the *Argo*:

> Peliaco quondam prognatae vertice pinus
> *dicuntur* liquidas Neptuni nasse per undas

> Once upon a time pine-trees, born on Pelion's peak, are said to have swum through Neptune's clear waters.

Not only is the poem's whole introductory section highly allusive, as was established in a fine article by Richard Thomas, which traced references in lines 1–18 to no fewer than five previous versions of the *Argo* story;[3] but also, in line 2, the word *dicuntur* 'are said to have . . .' draws attention to this very quality of allusiveness. 'Are said [in tradition]', but also, specifically, 'are said [in my literary predecessors]': the hinted 'footnote' underlines the allusiveness of the verses, and intensifies their demand to be interpreted *as* a system of allusions.[4]

And Ross's phrase 'Alexandrian *footnote*' catches it just right. *Dicuntur* is not of course a real footnote or scholium, such as one would find in Crassicius' commentary on Cinna's *Zmyrna* or in Servius' commentaries on Virgil; but it does very precisely mimic the citation style of a learned Latin commentary.[5] What emerges, then, is a trope for the poet's allusive activity, a figurative turn: the poet portrays himself as a kind of scholar, and portrays his allusion as a kind of learned citation (citation, it may be, with a distinctly polemical edge[6]). This figuring of allusion as scholarly activity, which often encodes a statement of alignment with the academic-poetic traditions of Callimachus and the Alexandrian library, has been taken up by modern academic critics with (understandable)

---

[3] Thomas (1982).

[4] So W.V. Clausen in *CHCL* 2.188; though for him the *gesture* towards allusive complexity is the crucial thing in *dicuntur*, not the actuality of the demand.

[5] As e.g. in Servius on *Aen.* 1.242 *hi enim duo* [Aeneas and Antenor] *Troiam prodidisse dicuntur secundum Livium . . .* 'for these two are said to have betrayed Troy according to Livy . . .'.

[6] Thus Thomas (1982), 146 ' . . . to demonstrate the importance of the poet's models, and often to indicate the superiority of his own treatment'. Other interpretative nuances too can be read into the 'Alexandrian footnote'. On play between 'footnoting' and 'distancing' see Horsfall (1990); response by Thomas (1993), 79–80.

enthusiasm, and has yielded a rich harvest of interpretation in recent years.

However, there are other ways too of metaphorizing allusion. The case-studies which follow will show two emphases. First, stress will be laid on the *range* of reflexive tropes used by Roman poets to describe and explore intertextual relations; second, whereas the *dicuntur* which is the 'signpost' of reflexive annotation in Catullus 64.2 is a sort of added, editorial intervention external to the events of the immediately surrounding narrative, the examples below will argue for the presence of signposting which is more deeply encoded, more fully integrated into its narrative contexts.

This is not uncharted territory any more,[7] and I begin by drawing brief attention to two already-published examples of reflexive annotation. First, here is Ovid's Ariadne in the *Fasti*, facing the unwelcome sequel to an act of abandonment famously recounted in (again) Catullus 64:

> 'en iterum, fluctus, similes audite querellas.
>   en iterum lacrimas accipe, harena, meas.
> dicebam, *memini*, "periure et perfide Theseu!"
>   ille abiit, eadem crimina Bacchus habet.
> nunc quoque "nulla viro" clamabo "femina credat";
>   nomine mutato causa relata mea est'   (*Fast.* 3.471–6)

'Again, o waves, hear a like complaint! Again, o sands, receive my tears! I used to say, I remember, "Perjured and faithless Theseus!" He has gone; now Bacchus incurs the same charge. Once again I will cry, "Let no woman trust a man!" My case is a repeat; only the name has changed'

> atque haec extremis maestam dixisse querellis,
> frigidulos udo singultus ore cientem:
> 'sicine me patriis avectam, perfide, ab aris,
> perfide, deserto liquisti in litore, Theseu?

---

[7] The first epigraph to my chapter, from Ricks (1976), 209, obliquely acknowledges an early debt of my own to a set of lectures heard in Cambridge in 1980. Ricks's distinctive emphasis upon self-referential tropes of paternity and inheritance in the allusions of the English Augustans is suggestively related to Roman allusive practice in Hardie (1993), 98–119.

> sicine discedens neglecto numine divum
> immemor a! devota domum periuria portas? . . .
> nunc iam nulla viro iuranti femina credat,
> nulla viri speret sermones esse fideles' (Catullus 64.130–5, 143–4)

And this last complaint did she mournfully utter, with chill sobs and tearful face: 'After carrying me off from my father's home, is this how you have left me, faithless, faithless Theseus, on the lonely shore? thus departing, all unmindful, without regard for the will of the gods, do you carry home the curse of perjury? . . . Henceforth let no woman trust a man's oath, or look for good faith in a man's speeches.'

In a now famous reading by Gian Biagio Conte, the word *memini* in the mouth of Ovid's Ariadne tropes the textual 'reminiscences' of Catullus 64 which inform her speech. Ariadne's 'memory' sets up some important tensions between narrative realism and intertextual continuity – tensions productively explored and theorized in Conte's monograph *Memoria dei poeti e sistema letterario* (for which this example becomes programmatic).[8] For now, I do no more than draw attention to the exemplification of my two chosen emphases. (1) The range of reflexive tropes used by Roman poets. (In this case, we find allusion figured, not as scholarship, but as memory – a metapoetic idea which may look back aetiologically to the mother of the Muses herself.[9]) (2) 'Signposting' of reflexive annotation which is more fully integrated into its narrative context than is that Catullan *dicuntur*. (*Memini* here is Ariadne's word, not the poet's. It is spoken 'in character'; and its operation as a signpost of reflexive annotation – its suspension of the artistic illusion – is covert rather than overt.[10])

My other preliminary example briefly revisits my own 1987 reading of the beginning of Ovid, *Amores* 2.6;[11] again a Catullan predecessor is involved.

---

[8] Conte (1985) 35–45; tr. in Conte (1986), 57–69. Among later discussions which take their bearings from these pages see Barchiesi (1986), esp. 93–102 ('Arianna e il suo futuro: *Heroides* 10.81–98'); Miller (1993); and (most spaciously) Barchiesi (1993).

[9] Mnemosyne: suggestive here is Miller (1993), 159–60.

[10] Note the intertextual irony which locates in Ariadne at *Fast.* 3.473 the very quality of mindfulness (*memini*) so signally lacking in her earlier lover at his moment of perjury: Catull. 64.135 *immemor a! devota domum periuria portas.*

[11] Hinds (1987b), 7; cf. 17–20, which pages can now complement sections 1 and 2 here.

> psittacus, Eois *imitatrix ales* ab Indis,
>   occidit . . .

The parrot, winged imitator from the Eastern Ind, is dead . . .

Corinna's engaging *psittacus* is modelled on Lesbia's famous *passer* or 'sparrow'; and it is called an *imitatrix ales* by Ovid not just because, as a parrot, its role in nature is to mimic, but because its role in the Latin erotic tradition is to 'imitate' that particular bird celebrated by Catullus. Again, the signposting is integral rather than added; and again a new area of metaphorical analogy for the intertextual relation is opened up. Opened up, perhaps – to take my earlier reading a stage further – into a question. *Can* we indeed read the parrot as a poet-analogue embodying the best of a *De imitatione*, or is the bird precisely constrained by its physiology to stand for the opposite?[12] Will Ovid's poem be a paradigm of creative imitation, or is there a danger that it will just 'parrot' its predecessor?[13]

2   Tropics of allusivity

For the first of two more concentrated discussions of allusive self-annotation, still staying with Ovid, I turn to the story of Narcissus and Echo in the *Metamorphoses*. A suggestive book by John Hollander has explored what Renaissance and post-Renaissance writers make of the myth of Echo as a way of thinking about poetic language.[14] What may now be noted is the extent to which they are preceded in this inquiry by Ovid himself. Here is Narcissus, at the very moment of death for love of his reflexion (*Met.* 3.499–501),

> ultima vox solitam fuit haec spectantis in undam:
> 'heu frustra dilecte puer!' totidemque remisit
> verba locus, dictoque *vale* '*vale*' inquit et Echo

---

[12] Cf. Myers (1990), 369n.8, 374.

[13] The programmatics of Ovid's parrot are taken up by Statius (*Silv.* 2.4) – and probably by Petronius before him (fr.45 Müller⁴, with Connors (1998), 47–9).

[14] Hollander (1981), x, modestly claims not to have the 'intuitive authority' to touch upon echoes *within* Greek and Latin poetry; but his parenthetic mention (13) of Val. Flacc. *Arg.* 3.596–7 as an 'allusive *vocis imago*' of Virg. *Ecl.* 6.44 ('*Hyla, Hyla*') could not be more germane to the present discussion.

His last words as he gazed into the familiar spring were these: 'Alas, dear boy, in vain beloved!'; the place gave back the self-same words. And when he said 'Farewell!' 'Farewell!' said Echo too

and here too, hovering between absence and presence, is the nymph Echo, expressing her own frustrated love for Narcissus in the only way she can. The last half-line offers an onomatopoeic depiction of an echo, with the correption of the vowel in hiatus giving a fading effect to the second *vale*: *valē valĕ*. But, more than this, the half-line constitutes an allusion to a half-line in Virgil's *Eclogues*, which has the same fading doubled *vale* (*Ecl.* 3.78–9):[15]

> Phyllida amo ante alias; nam me discedere flevit
> et 'longum, formose, *vale, vale,*' inquit, '*Iolla*'

> Phyllis I love beyond all; for she wept at my leaving, and said 'A long farewell, farewell, my lovely Iollas!'

As a character in Ovid's story, the nymph in *Met.* 3.501 echoes the *vale* uttered by Narcissus; but the further reverberation which exists between these two *vale*s and the two *vale*s uttered in the Virgilian poem casts Echo in another role: through her name she becomes the annotator, precisely, of an intertextual 'echo'.

And there may be a sequel, or rather an anticipation. This annotated echo at the end of the Narcissus episode can be related, I think, to a very recognizable but less obviously self-reflexive allusion at the very beginning of the Narcissus episode.[16]

> namque ter ad quinos unum Cephisius annum
> addiderat poteratque puer iuvenisque videri:
> *multi illum iuvenes, multae cupiere puellae;*
> sed (fuit in tenera tam dura superbia forma)
> *nulli illum iuvenes, nullae tetigere puellae*   (Ovid, *Met.* 3.351–5)

---

[15] By this period the normal pronunciation of the word was *valĕ*; so that in each pair the first *vale*, in which the final vowel retains its original quantity under the ictus, can be felt to be as instrumental as the second in setting up the special effect: cf. Clausen (1994) on *Ecl.* 3.79.

[16] For the ready recognizability of this allusion cf. Rosati (1983), 28n.63 and Farrell (1991), 12, each noting the suggestiveness of the Catullan flower (62.39 *ut flos*) *vis à vis* the metamorphosis awaiting Narcissus.

For Narcissus had reached his sixteenth year and might seem either boy or man. Many youths, many girls sought him; but in that delicate form was pride so stiff that no youths, no girls touched him

> ut flos in saeptis secretus nascitur hortis . . .
> *multi illum pueri, multae optavere puellae:*
> idem cum tenui carptus defloruit ungui,
> *nulli illum pueri, nullae optavere puellae:*
> sic virgo, dum intacta manet, dum cara suis est . . .
>
> ut vidua in nudo vitis quae nascitur arvo . . .
> *hanc nulli agricolae, nulli coluere iuvenci:*
> at si forte eadem est ulmo coniuncta marito,
> *multi illam agricolae, multi coluere iuvenci:*
> sic virgo dum intacta manet, dum inculta senescit
>
> (Catullus 62.39, 42–5, 49, 53–6)

As a flower grows up secretly in an enclosed garden . . . many boys, many girls desire it; when the same flower sheds its petals, nipped by a fine nail, no boys, no girls desire it: so a maiden, while she remains untouched, the while is she dear to her own . . .

As an unwedded vine which grows up in a bare field . . . no farmers, no oxen tend it: but if perchance it be joined in marriage to the elm, many farmers, many oxen tend it: so a maiden, while she remains untouched, the while is she ageing untended.

Commentators have repeatedly remarked on the fact that *all* the language in Ovid's episode of Narcissus and Echo is suggestively suffused with local verbal responses and 'echoes' – not just the actual conversations between Narcissus and Echo. Here, in the opening account of how the young Narcissus spurns his suitors, is a pair of echoing lines (*Met.* 3.353, 355);[17] and, more than that, these lines constitute an intertextual echo of a pair of echoing lines in a marriage hymn of Catullus (62.42, 44); and Catullus' echoing lines are themselves in echoing responsion with another pair of echoing lines within the Catullan marriage hymn itself (62.53, 55). Even before her entry into the Ovidian story, the figure of Echo has already made herself heard, albeit less explicitly than in *Met.*

[17] Thus far Rosati (1983), 28, in an excellent discussion: 'i vv. 353 e 355 . . . introducono un motivo che, semanticamente e formalmente, costituisce la chiave di lettura dell' intero episodio.'

3.501: echo as the trope of mannered repetition, within texts and between texts.

There is another way of looking at this too. If we turn things around, and take our bearings here from the Catullan text rather than from the Ovidian one, a competing (or complementary) trope may emerge. Catullus 62 is a *tour de force* of amoebean poetry, with lines 42/44 in strict responsion with lines 53/55. By eliciting such a close response at *Met.* 3.353/355, Catullus' pairs of lines in effect transmit their amoebean pattern from the text to the intertext: viewed from a Catullan (as opposed to an Ovidian) vantage-point, the relationship figures itself not as echo, but as a kind of intertextual modulation of amoebean song.[18]

Of course, it is Ovid who has made this Catullan vantage-point available. It is not surprising that the poet reprimanded as *nimium amator ingenii sui*[19] should provide so many good examples of allusive self-annotation. However, Ovid has no monopoly on the mannerism; and the second of this section's two case-studies turns to the more darkly exuberant tropes of Lucanian allusivity. Ever since the publication of Emanuele Narducci's article 'Il tronco di Pompeo' in 1973, the following correspondence has been a *locus classicus* for discussion of Lucan's intertextual engagement with Virgil:

> hunc ego, fluminea deformis truncus harena
> qui iacet, *agnosco* . . . (Lucan 1.685–6)

Him I recognize, that disfigured trunk lying upon the river sands

> . . . iacet ingens litore truncus,
> avulsumque umeris caput et sine nomine corpus
> (Virgil, *Aen.* 2.557–8)

He lies a mighty trunk upon the shore, the head torn from the shoulders, a nameless corpse.

The mutilated trunk of Pompey in *De Bello Civili* 1 alludes to the mutilated trunk of Priam in *Aeneid* 2. However, what gives this correspondence its real edge is that the trunk of Priam in *Aeneid* 2 seems *already*

---

[18] Discussion with Patricia Rosenmeyer and Charles Witke in 1990 helped this paragraph.
[19] Quint. *Inst.* 10.1.88 'too much in love with his own talents'.

itself to be an allusion to the trunk of Pompey. On the interpretation famously recorded by Servius on *Aen.* 2.557, it was from Pompey's death and mutilation that Virgil drew his Priam vignette in the first place:

> **iacet ingens litore truncus:** Pompei tangit historiam, cum 'ingens' dicit, non 'magnus'

> ... saying '*ingens*', not '*magnus*', he touches upon the story of Pompey [the Great].

Servian interpretations are not always to be taken at face value; but Narducci's documentation of the early-established conjunction of Pompey and Priam in the exemplary repertoire combines with Angus Bowie's recent arguments from the internal Virgilian context to offer compelling support to this long-favoured hunch.[20]

Now, after noting the basic affinity between these two passages in which a *truncus* lies (*iacet*) upon a shore, Narducci immediately goes on to suggest a more profound affinity between the Virgilian passage and the *later* Lucanian passage, at 8.698–711, in which the trunk of Pompey is actually present in the narrative – rather than merely prophesied, as in the Lucan 1 passage. But my interest here is in the Lucan 1 correspondence itself, a paradigm case of reflexive annotation. 'Him I recognize,' cries the frenzied matron who is the author of the grim civil war prophecies at 1.678ff., 'that disfigured trunk lying upon the river sands': *hunc ego ... agnosco. Whom* does she 'recognize'? As a prophet, she recognizes Pompey, of course, who will lie decapitated where the river Nile meets the sea twenty months and seven books of *De Bello Civili* later. But as a reflexive annotator, engaged in another kind of vatic interpretation,[21] she recognizes Priam – dramatizing our own realization, as readers, that we too have seen this decapitated trunk before: in the second book of the *Aeneid*.

Allusion troped as recognition, a signpost integral to the narrative: but we can press Lucan's reflexive annotation a little harder. How does one 'recognize' a corpse which is 'nameless', a *sine nomine corpus*? On an

---

[20] Narducci (1979), 44–7, with Cic. *Tusc.* 1.85–6 and *Div.* 2.22; Manil. 4.50–65, esp. 50 and 64; Bowie (1990). See also Moles (1983).

[21] On associations between prophetic and poetic vision in Lucan cf. O'Higgins (1988), 208–26; Masters (1992), index s.v. *vates*. For vocabulary of recognition in more straightforward Roman discussions of allusion, cf. chapter 2, section 2.

intertextual reading, Virgil's *sine nomine* deepens the paradox of Lucan's *agnosco*;[22] and also, *agnosco* exerts its own interpretative pressure on *sine nomine*, so that we may begin to wonder whether Virgil's phrase is itself already a reflexive annotation of his own pre-Lucanian borrowing from Roman history. A corpse without a name, says Virgil – is it Priam, or is it Pompey? Who can tell the difference? And we, as readers of Virgil, whose trunk should *we* recognize in the *Aeneid* 2 passage? Priam's, which lies *in* the text, or Pompey's, which lies *behind* it? 'Recognition' is all very well; but in this case it is no more than the prelude to interpretation.

Let me risk one final application of pressure. The Lucanian trunk is *deformis*, 'deformed', 'disfigured' – but also, perhaps (through word-play), characterized by *shifts* of form or figure: from Pompey to Priam, and back again to Pompey. The Virgilian trunk, in contrast, is *ingens*, 'mighty' – but also, perhaps, through Virgil's favourite etymology from **ingenens* (cf. *gigno*), 'in-born', 'innate': innate to Priam . . . or to Pompey?[23]

3   Reversing the trope

Where is an inquiry like this to proceed next? The assumptions behind my category of 'reflexive annotation' perhaps need to be tested within some larger theoretical perspectives. I could shift the balance of power away from the poet and towards the reader, and argue that, for all the intense authorial control which it presupposes, allusive self-annotation, like any other aspect of poetic meaning, is always, in practice, something (re)constructed *by the reader* at the point of reception.[24] This could lead to a more radical formulation, namely that *all* allusions, at the moment in which they are apprehended as such, incorporate an element of self-annotation, in that just to recognize an allusion, any allusion, is to hear in it the affirmation 'Yes, I *am* an allusion' – within, or besides, all the other things which it may be saying.

Another way to test the assumptions behind my discussion thus far is

---

[22] A moment of 'allusività antifrastica', and a complement to Narducci's exploration of the related paradox of recognizability at Lucan 8.710–11.

[23] On this etymology as underlying Virgilian uses of *ingens* see Mackail (1912), picked up by Ross (1987), index s.v. '*ingens*'; cf. Keith (1991).

[24] On the interpretative issues thus raised, cf. (more fully) chapter 2, section 5.

to problematize the hierarchy of 'tenor' and 'vehicle' in all the figures of allusive self-annotation explored in sections 1 and 2. I want to pursue this not uncomplicated idea, first with an example already adduced and then with a new one. In keeping with the agenda of this book, my account of the aforementioned figures has in every case treated *allusion* as the underlying idea or 'tenor', and *scholarship, memory* etc. as metaphorical 'vehicles' for that idea.[25] But (to return to the example of Ovid's Ariadne, invoked earlier) why assume that in *Fast.* 3.471–6 *memory* is really a way of talking about *allusion*, rather than *allusion* really being a way of talking about *memory*? If the Ariadne correspondence had been cited in a book about memory, rather than in a book about allusion, it might have seemed more natural to read the trope the other way around – to reverse the direction of explanation. Why, in other words, should it be taken as read that, in the metaphorical relationship between Ovid's allusion and Ariadne's memory at *Fast.* 3.471–6, the former functions as the primary field and the latter as the secondary field of signification – rather than *vice versa*?[26] This is a way of looking at things which is by no means alien to Conte's own finely theorized account of the Ariadne speech. However, to see more clearly why it may be useful thus to unpack the language of allusive self-annotation, let us consider a fresh example.

In the sixth book of Virgil's *Aeneid*, Aeneas and the Trojans make their way inland from the shores of Cumae to seek wood for the funeral pyre of Misenus (*Aen.* 6.179–82):

> itur in antiquam silvam, stabula alta ferarum;
> procumbunt piceae, sonat icta securibus ilex
> fraxineaeque trabes cuneis et fissile robur
> scinditur, advolvunt ingentes montibus ornos

Into an ancient forest goes their way, high home of beasts. Down drop the pitch-pines, the ilex echoes struck with axes; beams of ash and fissile oak are cleft by wedges; they roll down mighty rowans from the mountains.

---

[25] On I.A. Richards's 'tenor' and 'vehicle' see e.g. Silk (1974), 8–13.

[26] My methodology here owes something to Kennedy (1993), 46–63, a treatment of 'love's figures and tropes' which experiments with the heuristic reversal of 'tenors of signification'.

We owe to Macrobius, *Sat.* 6.2.27 the opportunity to compare this
tree-felling scene with its archaic Roman epic model at Ennius, *Ann.*
175–9 Sk. (with which it engages more concentratedly than with the
passages' common Homeric forebear at *Iliad* 23.114–20):

> incedunt arbusta per alta, securibus caedunt,
> percellunt magnas quercus, exciditur ilex,
> fraxinus frangitur atque abies consternitur alta,
> pinus proceras pervortunt: omne sonabat
> arbustum fremitu silvai frondosai

> They pass among the high groves, and hew with axes; they strike
> down great oaks; the ilex is chopped; the ash is shattered and the high
> fir laid low; they overturn lofty pines: the whole grove echoed with the
> leafy forest's din.

For twentieth-century critics, this pair of passages has become a test-case
for comparison and contrast between Virgil's and Ennius' epic styles.[27]
There is more than just the bare fact of the survival of the Ennian
passage to privilege the comparison. First, the very excessiveness of the
preparations for Misenus' funeral[28] invites interpretation of the *Aeneid*
passage as a display piece of rhetorical emulation. Second, the Virgilian
passage can be argued to *invoke* its archaic model with a programmatic
gesture of reflexive annotation in its opening phrase.

> itur in antiquam silvam . . .

Silva is used metaphorically in various contexts in Latin to represent
ὕλη, in the sense 'matter', 'mass of material', 'raw material' (for which
the more normal word is *materia*):[29] so, in Cicero, of the orator's debt to
philosophers' discussions, *Orat.* 12 *omnis enim ubertas et quasi silva
dicendi ducta ab illis est* 'all richness of style, and what may be called the
silva of oratory is derived from them'; so too, in Suetonius, of the legacy
of Probus, *Gram.* 24 *reliquit . . . non mediocrem silvam observationum
sermonis antiqui* ' . . . no mean *silva* of notes on ancient usage'. It is
precisely as *antiqua silva*, in this sense, that the Ennian passage is laid

---

[27] Williams (1968), 263–7; most recently, Goldberg (1995), 83–5 with bibl.
[28] See esp. Skutsch (1985) on Enn. *Ann.* fr. 175–9.
[29] See Coleman (1988), xxii–xxiii; *OLD* s.v. 5.

under contribution by Virgil here in *Aen.* 6.179–82. *Itur in antiquam silvam*: on this interpretation the allusion includes its self-annotation; the epic project of the poet is seen to move in step with the epic project of the hero.[30] As Aeneas finds his *silva*, so too does Virgil: the *tour de force* of allusion to poetic material from the *Aeneid*'s archaic predecessor, the *Annales*, is figured as a harvest of mighty timber from an old-growth forest – in a landscape (that of *Aeneid* 6) charged with associations of awe and venerability.

Here, then, is one strikingly metapoetic way of reading the figural relationship in this intertextual nexus: the landscape of ancient Italy serves to metaphorize a literary encounter between the poet of the *Aeneid* and his archaic predecessor in the Roman epic tradition. However, if this direction of explanation suits the emphasis of my chapter (and book) thus far, a more orthodox decorum of narrative representation might reasonably take the opposite approach: that is, it would treat the primordial landscape as the tenor (or primary field of signification) and the poetic tradition as the vehicle (or secondary field), not *vice versa*. Two ways of reading the allusion: which is to be preferred? Aeneas' intervention in an ancient Italian landscape as a metaphor for Virgil's intervention in archaic Roman poetry, or Virgil's intervention in archaic Roman poetry as a metaphor for Aeneas' intervention in an ancient Italian landscape?

The best answer, perhaps, will be one which refuses to treat the choice as a disjunctive one. The richest reading of the passage, the reading most fully responsive to the *Aeneid*'s many-layered explorations of pastness, is surely one which can admit the possibility of proceeding in both these directions simultaneously. In such a reading, as in Philip Hardie's readings of the dynamics of (post-)Augustan epic tradition, and as in Thomas Greene's generous vision of analogous kinds of imitation in the Renaissance, 'history, time and intertextuality' can all find themselves thematized in an event of intense reflexivity which, rather than just turning the poetry in on itself, opens it out into a referentiality which is

---

[30] The point is not made in the standard discussions; but it is not lost on Masters (1992), 25–9, in a superb treatment of Caesar's epic tree-felling at Massilia in Lucan 3.399–452. Many will think too of Mynors's intuitively apt quotation of *itur in antiquam silvam* to inaugurate his account of the Virgilian manuscript tradition in the Oxford Classical Text.

simultaneously self- and other-directed.[31] What better way to resolve the question of hierarchy raised at the beginning of this discussion?

It may be possible to take the figural reciprocity here a stage further. In a fine account of ethical undercurrents in this tree-felling scene within his 1988 article 'Tree violation and ambivalence in Virgil', Richard Thomas moves from the idea of awe to the idea of potential violation: 'There is in the words *itur in antiquam silvam, stabula alta ferarum* (179) a note of empathy and animism not found in Virgil's models, and the words *antiquam silvam* imply that the woods could be numinous, and that we are dealing with the disruption of an old order – that there are two sides to Aeneas' civilizing.'[32] Let us embrace this move; but let us also consider embracing the added resonance which it gains when, adducing the self-annotation in *Aen.* 6.179, we allow the hero's name to shade into the poet's, and another kind of 'old order' to come under threat. More than a century after the composition of the *Aeneid* Quintilian was to write (*Inst.* 10.1.88) *Ennium sicut sacros vetustate lucos adoremus* 'we should venerate Ennius as we do groves hallowed by age'; and the sacrosanctity of archaic poetry was a familiar idea in Virgil's own time (cf. Horace, *Epist.* 2.1.54).[33] In such a context, the idea of 'violation' may have its metapoetic dimension too. Qualms about Aeneas' disruption of his *antiqua silva* can induce qualms about Virgil's disruption of *his* – and *vice versa*: such, perhaps, is the effect of the movement across tropes here, a movement which might be described as meta-metaphoric, or (in a modern application of the term) 'transumptive'.[34]

A similar kind of mutuality can be discovered in the case of an Ovidian allusion to Ennius which is paired with the discussion of Ovid's Ariadne in Conte's *Memoria dei poeti*.[35] In the penultimate book of the *Metamorphoses* Mars reminds Jupiter of a long-standing promise to make Romulus into a god (*Met.* 14.812–16):

---

[31] Hardie (1993) *passim*; Greene (1982), esp. 52–3 (from which the quotation comes). For analogous approaches to Hellenistic literature see Bing (1988), 49–90; Goldhill (1991), 284–333.

[32] Thomas (1988b), 268.

[33] Both passages to be cited again below in chapter 3, section 2.

[34] In using the term (first attested at Quint. *Inst.* 8.6.37), I draw on modern reappropriations by Hollander (1981), 113–49, and Barkan (1991), 41–8, two difficult but rewarding discussions.

[35] Conte (1986), 57–9 (in the English translation).

'tu mihi concilio quondam praesente deorum
(nam memoro memorique animo pia verba notavi)
"unus erit quem tu tolles in caerula caeli"
dixisti: rata sit verborum summa tuorum!'
adnuit omnipotens . . .

'Once, in full council of gods, you said to me (I recorded the gracious words in my memory's seat, and now remind you) "There will be one whom you will raise to heaven's azure blue." Let the fullness of your words be ratified!' Omnipotent Jove nodded his assent.

The words of Jupiter, as quoted back at him by Mars, are also, verbatim, the words of Ennius, in whose *Annales* Jupiter's promise was 'first' made (54–5 Sk.):

'unus erit quem tu tolles in caerula caeli
templa'

As Conte observes, the citation of Ennius has an *authenticating* function in Ovid's text. But what is being authenticated, and by whom? On one kind of reflexive reading (which takes its cue from Conte), the passage uses the idea of Ennius' poetic authority to underwrite, figuratively, an appeal to the divine authority of Jupiter; on another (which takes its cue from my sections 1 and 2) the passage uses the idea of Jupiter's divine authority to underwrite, figuratively, an appeal to the poetic authority of Ennius.[36] These two ways of reading the trope encapsulate a tension between two kinds of authority in epic, the theological and the literary historical.[37] In the cosmos of Roman epic discourse, is the apotheosis of Romulus something guaranteed by Jupiter – or by Ennius? Again, perhaps, the richest answer is 'by both'.

Like Ariadne's *memini*, Mars' parenthesis at *Met.* 14.813 *(nam memoro memorique animo pia verba notavi)* tropes the succeeding Ennian allusion as, precisely, a 'memory'.[38] For Mars, and also for Ariadne

---

[36] Conte's readings here can all be associated with (though not reduced to) the first of my formulations; my second formulation opens up a line of enquiry explicitly disavowed by Conte (1986), 59.

[37] Cf. Feeney (1991) *passim.*

[38] The memory is not *quite* verbatim: Ovid's Mars drops the enjambed *templa* 'precincts', and so leaves the Ennian 'quotation' in 814 incomplete. May one read an arch acknowledgement of this into his immediately succeeding words (815): *rata sint verborum summa tuorum?*

(to return to this section's point of departure), let us now assert the mutuality of the figural relationship thus established. Mars' and Ariadne's memories function as figures for Ovid's acts of allusion to Ennius and to Catullus; but also, Ovid's acts of allusion to Ennius and Catullus function as figures for Mars' and Ariadne's memories.

How far are the terms of such figural relationships to be generalized? If we envisage *Fast.* 3.471–6 as a mutual exploration not just between Ovid's allusion and Ariadne's memory, but between allusion and memory themselves; if (as indeed was adumbrated in section 2) we read certain effects in Ovid's *Narcissus and Echo* as associating allusivity not just with the echoic utterances of one mythical nymph but with the echoic element in discourse itself; if we read *agnosco* at Lucan 1.686 as bringing into dialogue, not just the prophetic and poetic dimensions of one particular moment of vatic vision, but the prophetic and poetic dimensions of vatic insight at large – if we admit such spacious possibilities, we shall have demonstrated (if such demonstration is needed) that the mannerism of reflexive annotation, as well as turning the art of allusion in on itself in virtuoso extremes of involuted self-commentary, is no less capable of reconnecting it with the 'great world'[39] which gave it form.

[39] I.e. Ricks's phrase, back in the first epigraph to this chapter.

CHAPTER

2

Interpretability: beyond philological fundamentalism

By 'parallel' I mean an accidental (and inevitable) linguistic confluence, occasioned by the fact that certain phrases, metaphors, and the like are merely a part of a society's or language's parlance and to that extent defeat any attempt to prove that a given poet's usage is motivated by any other instance of the phenomenon.

(Richard Thomas, 'Virgil's *Georgics* and the art of reference', 174n.12)

Readers or imitators (also 'a type of reader) who approach the text are themselves already a plurality of texts and of different codes, some present and some lost or dissolved in that indefinite and generic fluid of literary *langue*.

(Gian Biagio Conte, *The Rhetoric of Imitation*, 29)

A Cold War exists between those who study 'allusion' and those who study 'intertextuality', and each term is a shorthand for a complex web of affiliation to, or distaste for, particular critical and methodological assumptions and those who hold them.

(Duncan Kennedy, *Greece & Rome* 42: 86)

1   Complexity and control

Chapter 2 begins once more with the launch of the *Argo*, but this time as a prelude to an immediate movement away from the kinds of allusive virtuosity considered in chapter 1. In 1982 (as noted at the outset of that discussion), Richard Thomas's article 'Catullus and the polemics of poetic reference' offered an unprecedentedly detailed analysis of the

introductory section of the *Peleus and Thetis*, which emerged thus as a
tour de force of neoteric self-fashioning by Catullus. Thomas's reading
isolated in the opening eighteen verses of poem 64 a complex system of
allusions to earlier versions of the *Argo* myth in Euripides, Apollonius,
Callimachus, Ennius and Accius. These allusions were all argued to be
precise and pointed, and to constitute a polemical engagement by the
poet with his tradition: the Catullan narrative was concerned to modify,
conflate, and incorporate prior treatments; in his self-presentation the
alluding author was seen (variously) to reject, correct, or pay homage to
his antecedents, acknowledging their importance but ultimately claim-
ing his own version as superior.[1]

This kind of reading was profoundly invigorating to Anglophone
Latinists in the early 1980s, eager as we were to speed the retreat of
lingering and debilitating charges of Roman derivativeness; and it has
continued to invigorate the reading of Latin ever since. The same spirit
informed another programmatically important intervention of these
years, David West and Tony Woodman's *Creative Imitation and Latin
Literature* (1979) – which wore the first two words of its title as a
triumphant oxymoron.[2]

However, there was an epistemological price to be paid. The new
vindication of the alluding poet's ability to exercise control over his own
tradition sharpened, and has continued to sharpen, an old philological
instinct to police and protect that idea of allusive control. At a time when
semiological approaches in the academy at large have increasingly em-
phasized the implicatedness of *all* literary language in intertextual nego-
tiations – an emphasis immediately discernible in the second of my
chapter's epigraphs – the mainstream of Latin allusive studies has moved
in the opposite direction, by circumscribing more narrowly the kinds of
intertextual event which merit study. The prescriptions set out in
Thomas's more recent 1986 article 'Virgil's *Georgics* and the art of
reference' are symptomatic here. Deploring the promiscuous citing of

---

[1] I paraphrase Thomas's conclusion at (1982), 163. To be sure, Thomas's exclusive
focus on the poem's opening verses leaves some broader implications unaddressed:
see Zetzel (1983), framed adversarially but perhaps better read complementarily;
and cf. my remarks on 'local' and 'systematic' approaches to allusion in chapter 4,
section 1 and chapter 5, section 3 below.
[2] Cf. West and Woodman (1979), ix: '*imitatio* is neither plagiarism nor a flaw in the
constitution of Latin literature. It is a dynamic law of its existence.'

literary 'parallels' in old-fashioned commentaries, 'whose importance goes uninterpreted and whose provenance seems to matter little', Thomas has argued for a rigorous distinction between the clearly defined allusion (polemically renamed 'reference': see below) on one hand, and the 'accidental confluence' of language on the other – with no grey areas or gradations acknowledged in between: 'Methodologically, there is one chief danger in a study such as this, that is, the problem of determining when a reference is really a reference, and when it is merely an accidental confluence, inevitable between poets dealing with a shared or related language.'[3] The occlusion of dynamics of language and literary discourse in the phrase '*merely* an accidental confluence' is notable. An occlusion not unlike Thomas's also characterizes the more nuanced, but still traditionally philological formulation of West and Woodman:[4]

> Similarities of word or thought or phrase can occur because writers are indebted to a common source, or because they are describing similar or conventional situations, or because their works belong to the same generic type of poem. Only patient scholarship and a thorough familiarity with the relevant material can reveal whether the similarities cannot be explained by any of these three reasons. In such cases we may be fairly certain that direct imitation of one author by another is taking place.

This is a fuller description of the variety of kinds of background noise which can get in the way of the rigorous study of 'direct imitations'. However, West and Woodman's discussion shares with Thomas's the assumption that for the student of allusion this noise *is* background noise, which can and should be tuned out whenever a *bona fide* allusion is tuned in. Furthermore, the conception of broader intertextual dynamics as a '*danger*' which *threatens* the study of allusion, explicit in Thomas's language, is a recurrent one: compare the preface of Kathleen Morgan's 1977 monograph *Ovid's Art of Imitation* (my emphasis): 'Only by establishing philological criteria for imitation can the *pitfalls* created by the thematic traditions of the genre be avoided.'[5]

Hence arises the 'philological fundamentalism' of my chapter title.

[3] Thomas (1986), 173, 174; another representative quotation forms this chapter's first epigraph.

[4] West and Woodman (1979), 195 (editorial epilogue).

[5] Morgan (1977), 3.

The recent quickening of some long-established critical procedures in
Latin literary studies has produced a quickening in our sensitivity to
allusive artistry; but it has also increased our susceptibility to a kind of
philological tunnel vision, by locking us more deeply into a poetic which
shows little interest in (and some nervousness about) situating clearly
defined allusions within broader dynamics of language and literary
discourse.[6]

The present chapter has two main objectives. First, it will seek to
extend into some less tidy areas the closeness of attention which recent
critics of Roman poetry have reserved for clearly definable allusions or
'references'; and second (and increasingly, as the chapter develops) it will
seek to suggest that the very distinction between 'reference' and 'acciden-
tal confluence' so anxiously enforced by Thomas and others is a prob-
lematic one – however pragmatically convenient it may be. The argu-
ment will not be against philology but against some consequences of
philological fundamentalism. The complex allusion described by recent
Latin criticism is a construct which has been repeatedly shown, in
practice, to have a good fit with some of the most distinctive features of
Roman poetic Alexandrianism: it needs recontextualization, not aban-
donment.

This discussion will involve along the way some exploration of the
rapprochement between traditional philology and semiology which is
(and long has been) fundamental to the work done on poetic imitation
by Gian Biagio Conte (already sampled in chapter 1).[7] That *rapproche-
ment* has been an enormously productive one; but it continues to cause a
few difficulties to readers on both sides of the 'Cold War' described in the
present chapter's third epigraph, partly because of an unresolved tension
in Conte's own original formulation of it. Like other semiological inter-

---

[6] Notable for its willingness to confront the characteristic occlusions is Lee (1971),
still one of the best accounts available of the strengths *and* limitations of the
philological study of allusion.

[7] Since the major impact of Conte's work on Anglophone Latinists dates from the
translation of a pair of key works into English in Conte (1986), it needs to be pointed
out that his systematic critique (and enlargement) of philological approaches to
allusion (esp. in Conte (1985), original ed. 1974) *predates* by several years all the
Anglophone discussions treated in this section. West and Woodman (1979) contains
no reference to Conte's 1974 monograph; nor does Thomas (1986), despite sharing a
starting point in Pasquali (1951). In contrast, Conte has held up his side of the
conversation throughout: cf. Conte (1981) on West and Woodman (1979).

textualists, Conte seeks to free his approach from reliance on the rhetoric of authorial intention and intersubjectivity;[8] but, as a full-time philologist concerned to locate his discussions within well-established Latinist debates, he tends to favour case-studies which remain persistently hospitable to the very terms which he would seek to sideline.[9] In my chapter's closing section, entitled 'The limits of intertextualism', I shall argue that this tension is a fruitful one, not evidence of methodological weakness.

My approach to these issues of methodological definition will be somewhat oblique. The classicist in Conte makes him a notably lapidary discourse-theorist, whose writing tends to capture an intertextual event in a moment of stillness, as a negotiation just completed. In contrast, my investigations of some limits of allusivity will seek to dramatize, often untidily, the *processes* of intertextual negotiation. My hope is that by allowing myself to focus on and speculate about the effort to connect, the conative element, involved in the reading of an allusion, I shall be able to do something to explore and to probe anew – through strategically chosen examples – the methodological pluralism which Conte's writing has established as an ideal.

2   'Allusion' and 'reference'

How does philological criticism envisage the relationship between alluding poet and reader? Thomas's version is again useful, in that it shows the regular working assumption in unusually high relief. Thomas rejects the traditional term 'allusion' in favour of 'reference', and his reasons are bound up with his definition of this relationship: ' . . . Virgil is not so much "playing" with his models, but constantly intends that his reader be "sent back" to them, consulting them through memory or physically, and that he then return and apply his observation to the Virgilian text; the word "allusion" has implications far too frivolous to suit this process.'[10]

---

[8] 'Intersubjectivity' rather than 'intertextuality' obtains when interpretation centres 'more on the personal will of two opposing authors than on the structural reality of the text': Conte (1986), 27.

[9] Sympathetic accounts of this tension in Conte (1986): Farrell (1991), 21–3; Barkan (1991), 42.

[10] Thomas (1986), 172n.8.

This is a tidy contract between author and reader, wherein the reader is enabled to take out exactly what the author has put in. The author is serious about the business of controlling his models (hence the banishment of the ludic connotations of the traditional label); and the reader (including the modern philological interpreter) is guaranteed a reward for being correspondingly serious about recognizing and applying those models (cf. West and Woodman's 'patient scholarship'). The strong association between poetry and scholarship in the Alexandrian and post-Alexandrian verse which serves as Thomas's laboratory (cf. chapter 1, section 1) guarantees and naturalizes the modern philologist's affinity with this ancient interpretative dynamic.

This account of the line of communication between author and reader, and the emphasis upon the author's sense of responsibility to both his models and his readers, has some affinities with the priorities and concerns of the strand of ancient criticism which is concerned to define 'borrowings', not against accidental confluences (that preoccupation is hard to find in ancient discussions), but against 'thefts'. Compare, for example, the well-known passage in which the Elder Seneca discusses the appropriation by Ovid of the Virgilian phrase (not, as it happens, in our texts of Virgil) *plena deo* (*Suas.* 3.7):[11]

> hoc autem dicebat Gallio Nasoni suo valde placuisse; itaque fecisse illum quod in multis aliis versibus Vergilii fecerat, *non subripiendi causa, sed palam mutuandi, hoc animo ut vellet agnosci*; esse autem in tragoedia eius: 'feror huc illuc, vae, plena deo'

> Gallio said that his friend Ovid had very much liked the phrase: and that as a result the poet did as he had done with many other lines of Virgil – not to steal it, but to borrow openly, with the intention of being recognized. And so in Ovid's tragedy you may read: 'I am borne hither and thither, alas, full of the god.'

For ancient and modern critic alike, the openness of the borrowing functions as a guarantee of the author's integrity: against plagiarism for Seneca, against imprecision for Thomas. As *palam* is to *clam*, so 'reference' is to 'allusion': a 'reference' is 'a specific direction of the attention'; an 'allusion', in the words of the *OED*, is 'a covert, implied or indirect reference'.

---

[11] Cf. Russell (1979), 12.

However, as these definitions serve to emphasize, there is a sense in which Thomas sells himself short in his polemical promotion of the term 'reference' over 'allusion'. A privileging of openness may do as a description of the disappointingly straightforward analyses of straightforward 'borrowings' typically found in ancient commentaries and rhetorical sources (like the passage of Seneca just quoted); but it hardly conveys a sense of the deeply encoded artistry which gives to complex Alexandrianizing allusion, and to the detective work of a modern philologist like Thomas himself, its real fascination. One of the reasons for the durability and continuing usefulness of 'allusion' as a description of this kind of gesture is precisely the teasing play which it defines between revelation and concealment.

Nor is openness in borrowing an absolute virtue even among the ancient critics. This can be illustrated by contrasting a pair of judgements in Book 5 of Macrobius' *Saturnalia* (the speaker in both cases is Eustathius). At *Sat.* 5.16.12, Virgil is indeed found guilty of violating the principle of open borrowing by (so to speak) sneaking a Homeric narrative vignette into the *Aeneid* disguised as a simile:[12]

> interdum sic auctorem suum dissimulanter imitatur, ut loci inde descripti solam dispositionem mutet et faciat velut aliud videri

> Sometimes Virgil disguises an imitation of his model author, by just changing the format of a passage copied from him, and making it look like something else.

That *dissimulanter* has a negative force here is made clear by Macrobius' resumption below: 5.16.14 *hoc quoque dissimulando subripuit* 'here too he has disguised a theft'.[13] However, from another ancient point of view this Virgilian manoeuvre might be cited as a wholly positive example of a principle which will often (though not inevitably) run athwart the principle of openness: namely, that the imitator should appropriate the imitation by avoiding too-faithful literalness in his rendering. So Horace, *A.P.* 131–5:[14]

---

[12] The passages under discussion are Hom. *Il.* 20.61–5, a glimpse of the underworld, and Virgil's corresponding simile at *Aen.* 8.243–6.

[13] For 5.16.12–14 as a piece of hostile criticism patched into a broader context of praise see Davies (1969), 357n.3.

[14] Cf. Russell's (1979), 12, statement of the best of both these ancient worlds: 'But acknowledgement, of course, must be combined with appropriation: a paradoxical

> publica materies privati iuris erit, si
> non . . .
> . . . verbo verbum curabis reddere fidus
> interpres, nec desilies imitator in artum,
> unde pedem proferre pudor vetet aut operis lex

> The common material will become your private property if you do
> not . . . anxiously render word for word, a (too-)faithful translator,
> or, in the process of imitation, put yourself in a tight corner from
> which timidity, or the rule of the craft, forbids you to move.

And the terms of disapproval applied to the Virgilian dissimulation at
Sat. 5.16.12–14 can be further qualified through appeal to a near-
adjacent judgement in the *Saturnalia* itself. At the beginning of chapter
18 Macrobius uses the adverb *dissimulanter* again – but this time *in praise
of* some more occult aspects of Virgilian imitation (*Sat.* 5.18.1):[15]

> ad illa venio quae de Graecarum litterarum penetralibus eruta nullis
> cognita sunt, nisi qui Graecam doctrinam diligenter hauserunt. fuit
> enim hic poeta ut scrupulose et anxie, ita dissimulanter et quasi
> clanculo doctus, ut multa transtulerit quae unde translata sint difficile
> sit cognitu

> I come now to passages which Virgil has dug out from the hidden
> recesses of Greek literature – passages understood only by attentive
> students who have drunk deep of the learning of Greece. For our
> poet's learning was not only thorough and painstaking, but also
> well-disguised and (one might almost say) covert, so that the source
> of many of his borrowings is hard to recognize.

The agenda is not quite the same as it was in chapter 16; but the
inconcinnity between these two Macrobian evaluations of dissimulation
remains a notable one.

The adverb paired with *dissimulanter* in this latter discussion – per-
haps with a hint of embarrassment? – is *clanculo*, the opposite of the

---

but essential point.' For the background to the Horatian discussion, see Brink
(1963–82) ad loc.

[15] An emphasis further clarified by the positive attitude shown to such occult artistry
throughout chapter 18: cf. 5.18.15 (arguing admiringly for a learned Virgilian
allusion to an ethnographic detail in Euripides) *in qua quidem re mirari est poetae
huius occultissimam diligentiam.*

Elder Seneca's *palam*. And so back to Thomas and to the descriptive limitations of 'reference'. The fact is that Macrobius' emphasis in *Sat.* 5.18.1 upon the difficulty involved in recognizing something which the poet has carefully concealed, and upon the tools to be brought to the job, is very much in sympathy with the spirit of Thomas's work on complex allusion[16] – and somewhat at odds with his preferred term, 'reference'.

Let us therefore, despite 'reference', affirm that what modern philologists are concerned with in the study of the complex allusion is a relationship between author and reader which can involve indirection as much as direction, concealment as much as revelation. However, this accommodation between variant labels is merely a preliminary. All the philological formulations set out early in section 1 share the presumption of Macrobius, *Sat.* 5.18.1 that an allusion is meaningful *as* an allusion only when the author knows exactly what it is that he is concealing and revealing; on those terms alone can the reader take up the implied challenge to interpret. What I shall do now is probe the limits of the allusive enterprise by seeking out examples in which, not only does readerly control become increasingly problematic, but that basic presumption of authorial control becomes problematic too. I intend to move the discussion towards a point where the interpretability of allusion is seen to break down – but to move gradually, so that along the way some interpretative possibilities will be glimpsed which would be lost if a rigidly polar choice were imposed between the clearly defined allusion on the one hand, and the 'mere accidental confluence' on the other. The paradoxical goal, then, is a more exact account of allusive inexactitude.

3   Fragments of a lover's discourse

The fear that 'accidental confluence' will invalidate a quest for a 'real' or 'certain' allusion is least likely to afflict the philologist in cases where a rare word or expression in one passage picks up a corresponding rarity in a predecessor passage, serving thus as an unequivocal marker[17] of allusion. There are abstruse lexicographical allusions to Homer in the poetry

---

[16] . . . as also is Macrobius' emphasis upon the prestige due to the interpreter of abstruse imitations; cf. Goldhill (1991), 289, on the active involvement of the reader in Alexandrian allusive writing: 'The process of recognition also invites a self-recognition as a knowing reader, a sharer of knowledge'.

[17] For the term 'marker', see Ben-Porat (1976).

of Alexandria which offer the ultimate assurance to the critic in their isolability and one-to-one specificity;[18] and in general it is a strength of classical philology to be sensitive to the allusive manipulation by poets of distinctive usages of diction, metre, and now (in an impressive book by Jeffrey Wills) figured word-repetition.[19] Such cases serve as a rallying point for the new poetics of allusive control. As we have seen, the philologist's working assumption (elevated in the fundamentalist version to dogma) is that the interpretability of an allusion *depends* upon its nearest possible approach to this kind of isolability. Morgan's list of 'philological criteria' in *Ovid's Art of Imitation* is useful and representative: 'similarity in choice of words, position of the words in the line, metrical anomalies, structural development of a particular passage, and other concrete evidence which can be linked to the work of an earlier author'.[20]

However, I should like to propose an axiom. There is no discursive element in a Roman poem, no matter how unremarkable in itself, and no matter how frequently repeated in the tradition, that cannot in some imaginable circumstance mobilize a specific allusion. This is a truth often suppressed by professors of Latin for reasons of pedagogy and (perhaps) peace of mind; but it is a truth none the less.

My first example in this section is an allusion usually interpreted as a clear one, even an 'open' one in the Senecan sense; but it offers a good initial point of access to some limits of clarity and openness. The expression of an inner conflict between love and hate is in itself not very remarkable. In some form, such a conflict has probably been expressed by a significant percentage of all language users in all cultures, past and present, endowed with vocabularies of self-awareness roughly compatible with our own. Yet when Ovid articulates it at *Amores* 3.11b.33–4 (1–2),

> luctantur pectusque leve in contraria tendunt
> hac amor hac odium; sed, puto, vincit amor

[18] For Alexandrian interest in Homeric *hapax legomena*, and for Roman interest in that interest, see Wills (1987), who finds the Theocritean *hapax* σκύφος (*Id.* 1.143; a kind of cup) alluding to the Homeric *hapax* σκύφος (*Od.* 14.112), and the Virgilian *hapax scyphus* (*Aen.* 8.278) alluding to both; a similar case at Farrell (1991), 242–3 (with further bibl.).

[19] Wills (1996), a ground-breaking work published too recently to be treated here.

[20] Morgan (1977), 3.

They struggle and draw my fickle heart in opposite directions, love now this way and hate now that; but I think the winner is love

we have no difficulty in recognizing an allusion to (and resolution of) Catullus 85:[21]

> odi et amo. quare id faciam, fortasse requiris.
> nescio, sed fieri sentio et excrucior

I hate and I love. Why I do so, perhaps you ask. I know not, but I feel it, and am crucified by pain.

Why has this proved so immediately and unanxiously identifiable as an allusion? After all, no lexicographically abstruse marker underwrites the Ovidian imitation. Nor (as just noted) can the sentiment itself be regarded as guaranteeing the Catullan poem as Ovid's model. Rather, the extensive work which has been done on precedents and parallels for Catullus 85 raises the spectre of the *topos* or commonplace[22] – than which nothing is more inimical to allusive specificity in the scheme of the philological fundamentalist. The inner conflict between love and hate can be paralleled in the lyrics of Anacreon (428 Page),

> ἐρέω τε δηὖτε κοὐκ ἐρέω
> καὶ μαίνομαι κοὐ μαίνομαι

Once again I love and I love not; I am mad and not mad

in the elegies of 'Theognis' (1091–4),

> ἀργαλέως μοι θυμὸς ἔχει περὶ σῆς φιλότητος·
> οὔτε γὰρ ἐχθαίρειν οὔτε φιλεῖν δύναμαι,
> γινώσκων χαλεπὸν μὲν ὅταν φίλος ἀνδρὶ γένηται
> ἐχθαίρειν, χαλεπὸν δ' οὐκ ἐθέλοντα φιλεῖν

My heart is troubled because of my love for you; for I am able neither to hate nor to love, knowing that it is hard to hate in the face of friendship, and hard to love when the other has no will for it

---

[21] A 'resolution' whose very facility (which has irritated many moderns) just might be a joke at the expense of those pedantic critics whose simplistic guidelines for allusive borrowing it so easily meets (cf. section 2 above).

[22] 'Der Gedanke stammt aus dem Inventar der erotischen *topoi*': Eduard Norden, quoted in Weinreich (1926), 52. More on *topoi*: section 4 below.

in the new comedy of Terence (*Eun.* 70–3),

> ... O indignum facinus! nunc ego
> et illam scelestam esse et me miserum sentio:
> et taedet et amore ardeo, et prudens sciens,
> vivos vidensque pereo, nec quid agam scio

What a sorry situation! Now I feel at once that she is wicked and I am wretched: I am both weary of her, and burning with love; knowing and fully sensible, alive and seeing it, I go to ruin, and don't know what to do

and even (of Athens' 'love-affair' with Alcibiades) in the old comedy of Aristophanes (*Frogs* 1425):[23]

> ποθεῖ μέν, ἐχθαίρει δέ, βούλεται δ' ἔχειν

She longs for him, she hates him, and then again she wants him.

I offer these parallels not to enter into a discussion about the conceivable or inconceivable influence of any one of these passages upon Catullus or (by extension) upon Ovid, but to dramatize the threat posed to the philological fundamentalist by the very possibility of coming up with such a list.

However, notwithstanding this glimpse of the dangers of accidental confluence, the allusion in Ovid, *Am.* 3.11b.33–4 to Catullus 85 has generally been read as a 'safe' one, which does not seriously infringe the philologist's criteria of interpretability. Why? First, even if it falls short of the ideal of lexicographical certainty, a strong case can be made that the words and antitheses of Ovid's couplet (and also of later couplets in the elegy) do indeed show specific responsiveness to the words and antitheses of the Catullan epigram (and also of Catullus' related epigrams on the love-hate conflict).[24] Second, the love-hate allusion enjoys the 'collective security' of being associated with another, even clearer Catullan allusion in its pair-poem, 3.11a (7 *perfer et obdura* 'persist and endure'; Catullus 8.11 *perfer, obdura*). Third, the model is one with which the poet of the *Amores* is 'demonstrably familiar' and generically

---

[23] ... itself an allusion to Ion, *TrGF* 19 F 44 – another day's work.

[24] *hac amor hac odium: odi et amo. sed, puto . . .* : *nescio, sed. . . . Am.* 3.11b.40 *et videor voti nescius esse mei* 'and I seem not to know my own desire': *nescio, sed fieri sentio. Am.* 3.11b.49–52: Catull. 72.7–8.

aligned.[25] Finally, the allusion is, intuitively, 'susceptible of interpretation'.[26]

Let me test the limits of this consensus by coming at the philologist's usual question about intelligibility from an unusual angle, and thus shifting the burden of proof. Not 'what markers are present which *allow* this to be interpreted as an allusion?' but 'what markers would need to be subtracted to *prevent* this from being interpreted as an allusion?'

What if Ovid's words and antitheses were just a little less responsive to Catullus' – so that (say) the similarities of expression between the Ovid and the Catullus were now on a par with the similarities of expression between the Ovid and the Terence quoted above? And what if the 'collective security' of the *perfer et obdura* were taken away? Would these subtractions remove the conditions in which the *Amores* passage could meaningfully be read as an allusion to Catullus 85 rather than as part of an uninterpretable pattern of 'confluence'? West and Woodman's terms (section 1 above) would now require such a disqualification; but that might be their and our loss. Ovid is writing in elegiacs (we have not subtracted that); and an argument can be made that the 'pull' of the elegiac genre as defined by an Augustan poet is enough *by itself* to privilege Catullus' previous formulation of the love-hate dichotomy above all other literary and subliterary instances, written and oral. For the poet of Corinna to set up a tension between hate and love *without* acknowledging the priority of the poet of Lesbia might even amount to a generic solecism. In the real world, a love-hate feeling may belong to everyone alike; but in the formal discourse of Roman elegy it is and always must be first and foremost *Catullus'* emotion. Such a formulation, in its appeal to the idea of interpretative community, both broadens and delimits: the claim is not that every conceivable reading of the Ovidian passage will be susceptible to this 'pull', but that every reading which acquiesces in the generic rules of engagement – including, most importantly, Ovid's own – will be susceptible to it.

A second example may allow us to consolidate and pursue this line of inquiry in a less hypothetical context. The exclamation *me miserum* is a

---

[25] Cf. *Am.* 3.9.61–2, 3.15.7; Hinds (1987b), 6–11.

[26] The quotations in my third and fourth points evoke 'two absolute criteria' offered by Thomas (1986), 174 for distinguishing between 'references' and 'accidental confluences'.

common piece of verbal furniture in a wide range of discursive situations in Latin. Yet when Ovid writes that exclamation at *Am.* 1.1.25–6,

> *me miserum!* certas habuit puer ille sagittas.
> uror, et in vacuo pectore regnat Amor

> Wretched me! That boy had sure arrows. I am on fire, and Love rules in my vacant heart

the commentary of J.C. McKeown argues for a specific allusion to Propertius 1.1.1–2,

> Cynthia prima suis *miserum me* cepit ocellis,
> contactum nullis ante cupidinibus

> Cynthia first with her eyes captured me, wretched, previously untouched by any desires.

His discussion is worth quoting at length for its unusual blend of philological give and take:[27]

> **me miserum!:** Ovid uses this exclamation 45 . . . times. It is not found in Vergil, Horace or Tibullus (*heu miserum!* at 2.3.78), in Propertius only at 2.33B.35 and 3.23.19. It is fairly common in Comedy and rhetorical prose; see *TLL* 8.1105.84ff . . . . Ovid favours the idiom because it helps to produce a lively style . . . Here, he is perhaps echoing and dramatising Prop. 1.1.1 *Cynthia prima suis miserum me cepit ocellis.*

We are far indeed from the realm of the Alexandrian lexicographical allusion. So, with the theatres, the speakers' platforms, perhaps the very streets of Rome resounding with the cry *me miserum*, how can a non-exclamatory Propertian *miserum me* make itself heard above the hubbub?[28] Again, we have to gauge the circumstances. The cry which is common in lively speech is actually uncommon in formal Augustan poetry before Ovid; in Ovid's opening, programmatic elegy the opening,

---

[27] As a critic with a strong sense of philological decorum, McKeown hedges his own note around thus: (1987–), II, 11 'Although there are no certain conceptual or verbal links between the two poems (but see on 25 *me miserum!*) . . . '.

[28] – not to mention the further noise generated by other, *non*-exclamatory utterances of *miserum me/me miserum*, above which Prop. 1.1.1 must be heard; an example lies as close at hand as Ter. *Eun.* 71, quoted earlier in another context.

programmatic elegy of Propertius (and especially its *incipit*) can be argued to be inherently foregrounded; other echoes of Propertius 1.1 have recently been heard in *Amores* 1.1, opening the way to some 'collective security';[29] the allusion may be interpretative, with Ovid suggesting that Propertius' phrase was *itself* designed to evoke the age-old cry *me miserum / miserum me*; and finally a specifically Propertian resonance would accentuate the appropriateness of *me miserum* as an emblematic catch-phrase for the moment here of Ovid's conversion to elegy – the genre persistently associated with lament by Roman poets sensitive to its perceived origins in funereal grief.[30]

I have given it my best shot; but in contrast with the case of the love-hate dichotomy in *Amores* 3.11b, there is no similarity of rhetorical configuration here with the proposed model; and, while my reading of McKeown convinces *me* that Ovid meant to do this, I doubt very much whether the entire community of his first readers heard the intertextual resonance, any more than it has been heard by the majority of his modern readers.

Embracing this uncertainty, I want to make another move away from philological security and toward the limits of interpretability – accepting McKeown's suggestion concerning *Am.* 1.1.25 for the sake of this part of the argument. McKeown notes that *me miserum* becomes an extremely common exclamation in Ovid (45 instances), though unused in the other major Augustan poets save twice in Propertius. Now, few would be rash enough to interpret all the later 44 Ovidian instances as allusions to the first instance in *Amores* 1.1, still less two-tier allusions[31] to *Am.* 1.1.25 and to Prop. 1.1.1 behind it. However, is it conceivable that the exclamatory phrase *me miserum* took root in Ovid's elegiac vocabulary – as it had not in the case of Tibullus or Propertius – partly *because* in *Amores* 1.1 he had given it that specifically Propertian, programmatically elegiac charge? Did that initial, very specific *repositioning* of the common phrase *me miserum* affect its connotation for Ovid thereafter, and encourage its later mobilization in his elegiac idiom – in ways of which the poet himself may not always have been fully or consistently conscious? Such a read-

[29] Keith (1992).
[30] Hor. *A.P.* 75 *versibus impariter iunctis querimonia primum* [*inclusa est*] 'verses unequally paired formed the setting first for lamentation'; Ov. *Am.* 3.9.3–4; Hinds (1987a), 103–4.
[31] For the category cf. Hinds (1987a), index s.v. 'allusion'.

ing may yield a handful of allusions interpretable in accordance with normal presumptions of authorial control;[32] but, more importantly for the present discussion, it names a more problematical field of semantic possibility which, once named, is hard to dismiss, but no less hard to pin down, in any or every instance in which Ovid utters *me miserum* in an amatory or an elegiac context. In such instances we would no longer be talking about allusion as it is usually talked about; we would no longer be talking about effects consistently compatible with a vocabulary of authorial control: but we *would* be taking notice of kinds of reverberation which will complicate even the tidiest of allusions, reverberations separable from the study of allusion only by a deliberate refusal to pursue the logic of the interpretative process.

That might seem to be a sufficiently close approach to the point of breakdown; but it is worth going one step further. Even gradations such as those just posited can ultimately be reconciled with traditional definitions of allusion, provided that these imperfectly controllable allusive reverberations are still regarded as isolable from a zone of zero-interpretability beyond them; in that way the philologist's fundamental distinction between allusion and 'accidental confluence' may yet remain operative. But what would this zone of zero-interpretability look like, in the case of *me miserum*? Let us venture beyond the limits of the (overlapping) systems of reference constituted by elegiac and amatory poetry for a glimpse.

Here is Cicero on the emotive subject of exile, with one among more than a dozen instances of exclamatory *me miserum* and *miserum me* in his speeches and letters (*Pro Milone* 102):

> O *me miserum*, o me infelicem! revocare tu me in patriam, Milo, potuisti per hos . . .

> O wretched me, o unhappy me! You, Milo, were able to call me back to my country with the aid of these gentlemen . . .

To the strict student of allusion, an instance of perfect irrelevance to the nexus centred on Ovid, *Am.* 1.1.25. And yet, like any utterance, this *me*

---

[32] Thus Apollo's *me miserum!* in pursuit of Daphne at *Met.* 1.508 might conceivably be readable as part of that (epic) episode's self-conscious recasting of Ovid's elegiac programme in *Am.* 1.1 – discussion of which centres upon the allusion in *Met.* 1.456 to *Am.* 1.1.5 (see Nicoll (1980)).

miserum comes with a rich freight of cultural resonance; and it may be instructive to resist, just for a moment, the philological sense of discrimination which hears it as mere noise to be tuned out in order for the allusive nexus centred on *Am.* 1.1.25 to be tuned in. Let us rather pause long enough to register some of that resonance – with the aid of Quintilian, who, as it happens, quotes this and other phrases from the peroration of the *Pro Milone* to illustrate the effective deployment of *miseratio* by a Roman orator (*Inst.* 11.3.170, 172):

> epilogus, . . . si [sc. ad iudices] misericordia commovendos [sc. est accommodatus, desiderat] flexum vocis et flebilem suavitatem, qua praecipue franguntur animi quaeque est maxime naturalis: nam etiam orbos viduasque videas in ipsis funeribus canoro quodam modo proclamantes . . .
> infinito magis illa flexa et circumducta sunt: *me miserum, me infelicem* . . . et *revocare tu me in patriam potuisti, Milo, per hos . . .*

> If the epilogue aims to rouse the judges to pity, the voice needs to be modulated to a tearful sweetness, which especially softens the heart and is most natural. For even orphans and widows in mid-funeral can be seen to have a certain musical quality in their cries . . . The following phrases from *Pro Milone* have infinitely greater modulation and longer-drawn harmonies: . . . (etc.)

The lesson (for our purposes) of Quintilian's commentary on *Pro Milone* 102 is that the 'hubbub' of *me miserum* to which I referred at the outset is actually composed of countless negotiations within and between the discourses of Roman culture. It is of such negotiations that the phenomenon which we call allusion is a special, stylized subset, a subset which allows the interventions of one self-fashioning voice, that of the alluding poet, to be privileged above other voices. Ovid is not of course alluding to the *Pro Milone*, not even indirectly, imperfectly or unconsciously. However, the discourses discussed by Quintilian form part of the cultural matrix from which Ovid's poetic voice emerges; and the ear which hears in the *me miserum* of a Ciceronian peroration a measure of rhetorical complicity with the demonstrative lamentations of women and children in Roman funeral processions becomes thereby an infinitesimally more sensitive instrument for apprehending intertextual trace-elements in the Ovidian lover's self-pitying and highly rhetorical cry of *me miserum* at *Am.* 1.1.25 – a cry framed, remember, within a genre which never ceases to be alive to its own funereal aetiology.

In short, the fact that language renders us always already acculturated guarantees that there is no such thing as a wholly non-negotiable confluence, no such thing as zero-interpretability. This is the basic insight of the semiological intertextualist; and in principle, as well as for the more practical dividends which it can offer, it should be embraced within the philological allusionist's enterprise, not treated as irrelevant or (worse) as a threat to it.

4   *Topoi* and accountability

If the 'accidental confluence' is regularly set in opposition to the clearly defined allusion in the philological scheme of things, another category traditionally opposed to allusion (not as uninterpretable, this time, but as interpretable within narrowly circumscribed limits) is the *topos* or commonplace. As normally defined, the *topos* is an intertextual gesture which, unlike the accidental confluence, is mobilized by the poet in full self-awareness. However, rather than demanding interpretation in relation to a specific model or models, like the allusion, the *topos* invokes its intertextual tradition as a collectivity, to which the individual contexts and connotations of individual prior instances are firmly subordinate.[33] Thus, in one of the most lucid treatments of the matter, Charles Martindale (as a classical Latinist) could begin his 1986 book on Milton by issuing a call to order to readers less familiar than he with the *topos*-traditions of ancient epic, urging that a clearer distinction be drawn between Milton's 'allusions', in which he alludes to particular models, and his adaptations of *topoi*, in which he plays with stock material, and in respect of which claims for specific allusivity could lead to misinterpretation.[34]

However (as, indeed, the Charles Martindale of the 1990s might be the first to argue), there are dangers of too easy an essentialism in such a firm distinction between allusion proper and participation in a *topos*. The

---

[33] For an influential definition and history of the *topos* as a category in philological criticism, see Curtius (1953), 70–1, 79–105.

[34] Martindale (1986), 4–11; among the more familiar instances of *topos*-adaptation discussed are 'thick as autumnal leaves' (*P.L.* 1.302) and 'if great things to small may be compar'd' (*P.L.* 10.306, et al.).

present discussion provides an environment hospitable to a small test of
the strength of the distinction, a test which will proceed by dismantling a
topos and putting it back together again.[35] As in the previous sections, the
aim will be to explore and to come to a better understanding of a durable
philological category, not to put a new category in its place.

In the course of his sustained exploration in *Saturnalia* 5 of Virgil's use
of Homer as chief archetype (5.13.40 *per omnem poesin suam hoc uno est
praecipue usus archetypo*), Macrobius has Eustathius juxtapose a passage
in *Aeneid* 6 in which the Sibyl declares herself incapable of compassing all
the crimes and punishments of the underworld, even had she multiple
tongues, multiple mouths and a voice of iron, and a passage in *Iliad* 2 in
which the Homeric poet uses almost the same set of terms to cast doubt
upon his capacity to extend his famous catalogue of Greek forces from
leaders to other ranks (*Aen.* 6.625–7, *Il.* 2.488–90, ap. *Sat.* 5.7.16):

> non, mihi si linguae centum sint oraque centum,
> ferrea vox, omnis scelerum comprendere formas,
> omnia poenarum percurrere nomina possim

Not if I were to have a hundred tongues, a hundred mouths, and a
voice of iron, could I compass all the forms of crime, or list all the
names of the punishments

> πληθὺν δ' οὐκ ἂν ἐγὼ μυθήσομαι οὐδ' ὀνομήνω,
> οὐδ' εἴ μοι δέκα μὲν γλῶσσαι, δέκα δὲ στόματ' εἶεν,
> φωνὴ δ' ἄρρηκτος, χάλκεον δέ μοι ἦτορ ἐνείη

But the multitude I could not tell or name, not if ten tongues were
mine and ten mouths, an unbreakable voice and a heart of bronze . . .

At this point in his disquisition Eustathius has reduced his interpretative
input to a bare listing of correspondences (5.3.15–17). Fleshing things
out for ourselves, we might provisionally agree on the basis of the data
given that this looks like a clear and specific allusion: 'Virgil preserves
the anaphora of the Homeric model (δέκα . . . δέκα), but for greater effect
changes the number from 10 to 100.'

My quotation comes from an actual modern commentary; but I cheat
a little. This is a note by Richard Thomas, not on *Aen.* 6.625–6, but on an

---

[35] More conventional accounts of the 'many mouths' *topos* than the one below are
available: e.g. Häussler (1976), 322–3.

identical line-and-a-quarter at *Geo.* 2.43–4, in which Virgil had earlier deployed, verbatim, the same configuration of tongues, mouths and voice to declare his unwillingness to embrace in his verse the totality of didactic lore on arboriculture.[36] More on the Virgilian duplication later; for now I stay with the *Georgic* version of the doublet to bring in another ancient witness. Scholia on *Geo.* 2.43[37] reveal the existence of an intermediate version of the 'many mouths' conceit, by Ennius (cited below as restored by Skutsch, *Ann.* 469–70):

> **linguae:** Homericus sensus Graeci poetae, sicut et Ennius:
> non si, lingua loqui saperet quibus, ora decem sint
> in me, tum ferro cor sit pectusque revinctum

> The idea is taken from the Greek poet Homer; so too Ennius: 'Not if I were to have ten mouths with which my tongue could have sense to speak, and my heart and breast were encased in iron.'

The allusive narrative becomes a little more complicated; but, if anything, there seems to be an increase in specificity and point. In *ferrea vox* Virgil modifies Homer's χάλκεον . . . ἦτορ by switching a metallic epithet from the heart to the voice; and it can now be seen that he incorporates an acknowledgement of Ennius, who had already changed that metal from bronze to iron. 'Virgil has conflated his two models' (Thomas again, on *Geo.* 2.44).

But there is more. Twin notes by Servius on the *Georgic-Aeneid* doublet plot into the picture an otherwise unknown passage of Lucretius:[38]

> **non ego cuncta meis:** Lucretii versus; sed ille aerea vox ait, non ferrea

> Verse from Lucretius; but he says 'voice of bronze', not 'of iron'.

---

[36] 'Unwillingness', not 'incapacity', a notable modification of what will emerge below as the usual emphasis, acutely interpreted by Thomas (1988a) ad loc. as laying claim to a specifically Callimachean virtuosity which *could* compass the totality but chooses not to: *Geo.* 2.42–4 *non ego cuncta meis amplecti versibus opto,* / *non, mihi si linguae centum sint oraque centum,* / *ferrea vox.*

[37] I quote *Brevis Expositio Geo.* 2.43; cf. *Schol. Bern.* ad loc.

[38] Serv. *Geo.* 2.42, with Lachmann's *aerea* for *aenea*; cf. Serv. *Aen.* 6.625 **non mihi si linguae centum sint:** *Lucretii versus sublatus de Homero* ('lifted from Homer'), *sed aerea vox dixit*. On attempts to place this passage in Lucretius see Farrell (1991), 232n.56, with bibl. too on the idea that it should be reassigned to Lucilius, scribal confusion between the two names being common.

What emerges from this *testimonium* (if reliable) is that Lucretius has already performed the modification of Homer which we were crediting a moment ago to Virgil: he has already switched the metallic epithet from the heart to the voice – but without following Ennius in changing the metal from bronze to iron. Our complex allusion now orchestrates three models.

For one last (extant) complication, we may return to Macrobius. In *Saturnalia* 6, Furius puts Eustathius' survey of Virgil's debts to Homer (discussed above) into direct competition with a survey of Virgilian debts to Roman predecessors (6.1.7): *quaedam de his quae ab Homero sumpta sunt ostendam non ipsum ab Homero tulisse, sed prius alios inde sumpsisse, et hunc ab illis, quos sine dubio legerat, transtulisse* 'As for certain of the things taken from Homer, I shall show that Virgil did not himself get them from Homer but that others before him had taken from that source and that Virgil (having certainly read their works) copied from them.' Among his examples is the following (6.3.6):

Homeri est:

οὐδ' εἴ μοι δέκα μὲν γλῶσσαι, δέκα δὲ στόματ' εἶεν

hunc secutus Hostius poeta in libro secundo belli Histrici ait:

non si mihi linguae

centum atque ora sient totidem vocesque liquatae

hinc Vergilius ait:

non mihi si linguae centum sint oraque centum

... Following Homer, the poet Hostius says in the second book of his *Bellum Histricum*: 'Not if I were to have a hundred tongues, as many mouths, and voices clear'. Hence Virgil says: ... (etc.)

It now turns out that the first move which Thomas (and implicitly Eustathius) credited to Virgil, the multiplication 'for greater effect' of Homer's ten mouths to a hundred, was anticipated in the *Bellum Histricum* of the epic poet Hostius (late second century BCE) at fr. 3. Note Furius' emphasis: Hostius follows Homer, Virgil follows Hostius, and the polemical point is that (therefore) Virgil does not follow Homer. However, an approach in terms of complex allusion will rather see Virgil as absorbing and transforming both Homer and Hostius – along with Ennius, *Ann.* 469–70 and the possible fragment of Lucretius.

Our initial attempt to read Virgil's 'many mouths' passage as a tightly controlled allusion is perhaps becoming a little problematic. Closer investigation has now yielded no fewer than four models, including the Homeric archetype; and that proliferation raises questions of emphasis and foregrounding which cannot all be answered as crisply as (say) Thomas was able to answer such questions for the *Argo* intertexts in Catullus 64. The permutations of markers linking Virgil's iron voice to Homer's bronze breast via Lucretius' bronze voice and Ennius' iron breast can indeed be plotted tidily, with every permutation leaving its isolable trace in the philological record – so that Thomas's note on *Geo.* 2.44 about Virgil's conflation of two models (Homer and Ennius) can be revised in Thomas's own terms into a description of an even richer conflation of four models. But, on the matter of the multiplication which increases Homer's ten mouths to one hundred, the first-quoted note by Thomas constitutes a small philological crisis. If interpretable allusion requires isolable markers or cues, then the multiplication of mouths can be used to talk about Hostius' allusion to Homer; but the priority of the Hostian passage robs the marker of its interpretability in respect of Virgil's allusion to Homer – unless we dodge the methodological bullet by positing blank ignorance of the Hostian passage on Virgil's part.

However, philological markers notwithstanding, it seems to me that Thomas's note on the multiplication deserves to be defended – at least as a reading of the *Aeneid* version of the doublet. Despite Hostius' priority (and with due caution expressed in view of the decontextualized state of his fragment), in the larger schemes of the *Aeneid* it is surely intuitively *right* to describe this as a moment at which Virgil is in dialogue with *Homer*, not with Homer and Hostius. However, such a reading necessarily involves a renunciation of philological fundamentalism in favour of a less tidy approach to the allusion, grounded not so much in isolable cues as in what may be called for now a broader and more dynamic sense of contextual appropriateness (on which more at the end of the section).

A further wrinkle. Michael Wigodsky conjectures on the basis of the blanket claim in the twin Servian notes ('*Lucretii versus*') that Lucretius too (after Hostius) anticipated Virgil in the 10-to-100 multiplication.[39] That would require us, and Virgil, to allow a Lucretian multiplication as well as a Hostian one to fade into the background as the Homeric

---

[39] Wigodsky (1972), 98–9, whose agenda is the promotion of the better-known Lucretius (or Lucilius: see prev. n.) over the 'minor epic poet' Hostius as Virgil's model for the 10-to-100 multiplication.

archetype is invoked, and 'capped', in *Aen.* 6.625–6. Fair enough: but can this same permission be granted in the case of the *Georgic* version of the doublet (the one on which Thomas actually comments) where, although the markers are identical, Lucretius may have a better claim to the status of archetype than Homer, given the generic affiliation of the earlier Virgilian work with didactic?[40] Granted, this new Lucretian wrinkle rests upon the evidence of Servius, a commentator notorious for his vagueness in delimiting allusive debts; but in methodological terms the important lesson is that an approach based on tight allusive control shows increasing vulnerability as problems and possibilities *of this kind* build.

Modern commentaries on Roman poetic texts face this sort of difficulty all the time. It is interesting that, of the two recent commentators on the *Georgics*, Thomas, who reads 2.43–4 as a precise and pointed allusion, can do so only by occluding some of the material which his own procedures would seem to require him to account for; whereas Mynors, who does name all the Republican passages attested by ancient Virgilian exegesis, avoids the discourse of allusivity altogether by presenting the passages as, in effect, the timeless record of a *topos*.

The usual philological solution to the kind of problem recreated above is to enact precisely this latter, reifying move. In other words, faced with a Babel of claims and counter-claims to specific allusive interpretability coming from untidily proliferating sources, the commentator capitulates, deciding that the motif in question is so common – such a *topos*, as the term has it – as to forfeit any potential to be treated as more than merely inert. Many philologists would argue for just such a capitulation in the case of the 'many mouths' motif; and they might cite the world-weary words of the satirist Persius to claim a warrant in ancient poetic practice for the move towards reification (5.1–4):

> *vatibus hic mos est*, centum sibi poscere voces,
> centum ora et linguas optare in carmina centum,
> fabula seu maesto ponatur hianda tragoedo,
> vulnera seu Parthi ducentis ab inguine ferrum

This is the poets' custom: to demand a hundred voices, to seek a hundred mouths and a hundred tongues for song, whether the piece

---

[40] Homeric and Lucretian claims at *Geo.* 2.43–4 are finely handled by Farrell (1991), 232–4.

em be a play for the tragic actor's sad gape, or a tale of the
ɹ Parthian pulling iron from his groin.

Variuɯ_ _c mos est: a cliché, a dead horse being flogged at an exhausted
Hippocrene.[41]

But this is a counsel of despair. Persius' characterization of the
'many mouths' habit of elevated poets does seem to support the idea of
the *topos* as an inert collectivity, and indeed to lend aid and comfort to
more general philological strictures which seek to limit the situations in
which significance should be attached to verbal and thematic recur-
rence in Latin verse, on the grounds that Latin verse works with a
limited number of words and themes. However, easy appeals to such
strictures seem to me to do scant justice to the characteristic dynamics
involved in the production and reception of elevated poetry in Rome.
A discourse which is as circumscribed as is Roman poetry in its choices
of genre, subject-matter and vocabulary is more sensitive, not less sen-
sitive, to the need to confront its past utterances. The so-called com-
monplace, despite our name for it, is not an inert category in this
discourse but an active one, with as much potential to draw poet and
reader into, as away from, engagement with the specificities of its his-
tory. Members of the Roman literary élite learned in school to declaim
on set themes such as the sacrifice of Iphigenia, or the deliberation of
the three hundred Spartans at Thermopylae, and to embellish their
declamations with expected topics like the details of a storm, or the
vicissitudes of fortune.[42] The immediate point of these exercises was to
make something new and fresh out of something well-worn; and the
way to excel will have been to engage actively with existing literary and
rhetorical versions of the given theme. Against Persius may be cited the
Younger Seneca, encouraging his addressee Lucilius to take on that
favourite poets' topic, a description of Mount Etna (*Ep.* 79.6):[43]

---

[41] We may infer from Persius' description that our extant list of 'many mouths'
passages is incomplete: no tragic instances are known to us.

[42] Sen. *Suas.* 3, *Suas.* 2; Winterbottom (1974) vol. 2, index II s.vv. 'descriptions of
storms', 'commonplaces on fortune'. My use of these analogies from rhetorical
practice is not intended to elide the distinctions between *topos* as a term of modern
philology and *topos* as a term of ancient rhetoric: see Pernot (1986).

[43] *hunc sollemnem omnibus poetis locum* (79.5): cf. Russell (1979), 5; Fantham (1982),
24.

condicio optima est ultimi: parata verba invenit, quae aliter instructa novam faciem habent

The last comer has the best situation. He finds the words to hand; differently arranged, they take on a new look.

More than that, Persius himself can be cited against Persius:[44] in the very act of characterizing the 'many mouths' as a cliché, the satirist executes his own brilliant swerve upon it (5.5–6):

'quorsum haec? aut quantas robusti carminis offas
ingeris, ut par sit centeno gutture niti?'

'Where is this going? What great gobbets of robust song are you taking in, that need one hundred gullets to strain?'

Suddenly the image of utterance has become an image of ingestion, and the hundred mouths, rather than singing out poetry, are swallowing it down their hundred gullets in bite-sized chunks: nothing could be farther from inertia than this programmatic co-opting of a favourite epic motif to the alimentary aesthetic of satire.[45]

A more promising way to talk about the toposness of the 'many-mouths' *topos* might be to characterize it, not in terms of allusive inertia, but, with the help of a key Contean distinction, in terms of a subordination of modelling *by particular source-passages* to modelling *by code*. In the defining illustration of Conte's powerful double vision of literary imitation, Homer functions for Virgil in the *Aeneid* as the 'modello-esemplare', i.e. 'as the model constituted by the accretion of a series of individual imitations'; but he also functions as the 'modello-codice', i.e. as 'the representative of the institution of epic poetry itself'. The former kind of imitation involves the 'reproduc[tion of] single *loci*', the latter involves the 'assimilat[ion of] rules and codifications'. 'Homer is often, indeed nearly always, Virgil's "exemplary model" (together with Apollonius of Rhodes, Naevius, Ennius, the Greek and Roman tragedians, and several other authors), but he is also constantly the "code model".'[46]

---

[44] My thanks to Dan Hooley for pointing me in this direction.

[45] At 5.26–9 Persius is ready to reapproach the motif on his own terms: cf. Bramble (1974), 8–9. At 5.189–91, in the satire's coda, the pattern of counting by hundreds makes one last surprise appearance – which distorts the terms of the *topos* almost, but not quite, beyond recognition: cf. Anderson (1982), 162–3.

[46] Quotation and retranslation of Conte (1986), 31, after (1985), 121–2; cf. also (1981),

All the discussions above of Virgilian and pre-Virgilian transform-
ations of the 'many mouths' motif, whether more or less tidy, involve
reading *Il.* 2.488–90 as inaugurating a system of cues – a code – for
expressions of epic countlessness. The permutations (of number, of
metal, of location of metal) are interpretable as negotiations within that
system rather than with the specific situations in the specific poems thus
drawn on (in the case of *Iliad* 2, muster of Danaan forces at Troy). In
other words, active modelling *does* occur here; but it is modelling by
code, not modelling by particular source-passage. On this formulation,
the toposness of the 'many-mouths' *topos* lies not in allusive inertia *tout
court*, but in the observance of a stable set of parameters (a *topos*-code)
within which endlessly active (and endlessly interpretable) allusive vari-
ation can be contained.

This is an enabling formulation (and one quite compatible with Mar-
tindale's accounts of Miltonic engagement with commonplace-tradi-
tions). However, having established it, I also want to put it to work by
destabilizing it a little. Observe that my Contean redescription of the
topos does not banish the appeal to inertia altogether, but rather relo-
cates it in a semiological appeal to the fixity of a *topos*-code. But how
fixed is that fixity? In my account of Virgilian and pre-Virgilian 'many
mouths' passages, it was notably easy to construct the iron voice,
bronze voice, iron breast and so forth as allusive permutations within a
stable code, because in the case of three of those passages (the Ennius,
Hostius and Lucretius) the *topos* is transmitted to us *as* pure *topos*,
stripped of all other contexts. However, if we turn our attention to the
interaction of *non-fragmentary* instances of the *topos*, can we be so sure
that the code itself will remain immutable under the pressure of a more
palpable and less circumscribable range of textual and intertextual
agendas?

Consider Ovid, *Tristia* 1.5.53–6, where the poet complains about the
plethora of woes, *mala*, which have beset him since his exile:

148. I offer the formulation 'modelling by particular source-passage' to gloss
Conte's 'modello-esemplare' because the usual translation, 'exemplary model',
deploys an English adjective with connotations which can be felt to cloud the
intended distinction with 'code model'. 'Example-model', though less elegant, is
closer to the required sense, viz model *qua n* particular *exempla* imitated. In a
related (but not identical) formulation of this double vision, Barchiesi (1984),
91–122, offers in the place of 'modello-codice' the equally efficient 'modello-genere';
cf. Conte-Barchiesi (1989), 93–6.

> si vox infragilis, pectus mihi firmius aere,
>> pluraque cum linguis pluribus ora forent,
> non tamen idcirco complecterer omnia verbis,
>> materia vires exsuperante meas

If I had an unbreakable voice, a breast stronger than bronze, and a plurality of mouths with a plurality of tongues, not even so could I embrace them all in words, for the material surpasses my strength.

Granted, we can get a good run for our money with the same analysis of permutations within a fixed system as was deployed for the Virgilian doublet. *Plura . . . ora, linguis pluribus*: the imprecision of the enumeration is readable as a precise comment on the prior history of the *topos*: more than Homer's ten, more than Hostius' and Virgil's hundred, more than the ten, hundred and thousand already deployed by Ovid in a microcosm of this *topos*-intensification played out in his own earlier *oeuvre* (*A.A.* 1.433–6, *Met.* 8.533–5, *Fast.* 2.119–20 respectively). *Pectus mihi firmius aere*: at one level the comparative *firmius* can underline the translation of the Homeric original ('like Homer's χάλκεον ἦτορ, only more so'); at another level, perhaps, it hints at what had previously been made of that Homeric original by Ennius ('Q: What is stronger than a breast of bronze? A: A breast of iron').[47]

However, here are two other interpretative directions, which in different ways put pressure upon the toposness of the *topos* as we are currently defining it. First, this *Tristia* passage can be argued to engage with *Il.* 2.488–90, not just as the archetype of the *topos*, but with attentive reference to its extra-topical particularities – not just as 'modello-codice' but also as 'modello-esemplare'. At the point at which the *topos* occurs, the elegy is about to shift into an extended and explicit *syncrisis* between Ovid's sufferings and those of Ulysses (1.5.57–84): thus the evocation of Homer's *Iliad* in 1.5.53–6 can be felt to anticipate and to set off the coming *tour de force* of allusion to Homer's other great poem, the *Odyssey*. In 1.5.57–8 Ovid will claim to outdo Homer's proverbially 'much-enduring' Ulysses in quantity of woes endured;

> pro duce Neritio docti mala nostra poetae
>> scribite: Neritio nam mala plura tuli

Learned poets, write of my woes instead of the Neritian leader's! for I have endured more than the Neritian

---

[47] This paragraph is indebted to a conversation with John Dillery.

in 1.5.53–6 he prepares for this by alluding to the famous passage in which Homer himself had acknowledged that epic quantifying is a difficult thing to do. Ovid even 'annotates' his allusive shift from the Iliadic catalogue of leaders to the *Odyssey* by the way in which he names Ulysses in the transitional couplet just quoted. Ulysses is envisaged, precisely, as a leader (*duce*); and he is given an abstruse geographical epithet (*Neritio*) which can be glossed from Ulysses' own entry in the Iliadic catalogue.[48] In sum, *Iliad* 2.488–90 is invoked not just as *topos*, but in its own (inter)textual particularity: Ovid has forced us to break down Martindale's confident distinction between the interpretative procedures respectively appropriate to commonplaces and to allusions.

A second kind of pressure can be applied if we take a closer look at some of the *Tristia* passage's most immediate predecessors in the timeline of the *topos* – paying attention now, not to the question of factor-ten multiplication, but to some less measurable considerations which were unavailable in the case of the fragmentary transformations adduced in connexion with the Virgilian doublet. None of the following suggestions is tidy; none can even begin to approach isolability (unlike the pattern of allusion to the *Iliad* just proposed); but cumulatively they may allow us to put some pressure on the very distinction between 'modello-codice' and 'modello-esemplare' – if (as in section 3 above) we are prepared to speculate for a while in the outer reaches of interpretability.

Ovid's earlier, thousand-mouth instance of the *topos* in the second book of the *Fasti* explicitly characterizes the poet as under strain because he is burdening an elegiac poem with weighty subject-matter (Augustus and his exploits) more appropriate to epic (2.119–26).[49] One might argue that this programmatic emphasis on generic difference resonates here in the later elegiac setting of *Tristia* 1.5, in which (as we have just seen) Ovid juxtaposes the *topos* with a strong hint that the proper poetic vehicle for his countless woes would be a sort of super-*Odyssey*.

In Ovid's hundred-mouth instance at *Metamorphoses* 8.533–5 (written, like the *Fasti* passage, in the years just preceding his exile), the *topos* expresses the countlessness of the funeral lamentations offered by his sisters to the dead Meleager. In terms of subject-matter, this is closer to

---

[48] *Il.* 2.631–2 αὐτὰρ ᾿Οδυσσεὺς ἦγε Κεφαλλῆνας μεγαθύμους, / οἵ ῥ᾿ ᾿Ιθάκην εἶχον καὶ Νήριτον εἰνοσίφυλλον 'Then Ulysses led the great-spirited Cephallenians, who held Ithaca and Neritus with its quivering leaves'.

[49] Cf. Hinds (1992), 82–5.

what Ovid is counting in *Tristia* 1.5 – *mala*, woes – than are any of the other commodities catalogued in the known previous history of the *topos*. Moreover, in the sense that Ovid pervasively figures the *Tristia* as a collection of funeral laments for a poet to whom exile was death, his accumulation here of his own sorrows finds an apt anticipation in the sisters' *tristia . . . dicta* 'words of sadness' (*Met.* 8.535) for Meleager.[50]

To venture even deeper into the shadows of exile as death, Virgil's version of the *topos* in *Aeneid* 6, voiced by the Sibyl, uses it of the countlessness of Tartarean crimes and divine punishments. Ovid repeatedly in the exile poetry portrays his sufferings as a punishment meted out to him for an alleged crime by a god-like Augustus. So does Virgil's prestigious intervention in the *topos* attract *Trist.* 1.5.53–6 in the direction of an association between Ovidian *mala* and hellish Virgilian *poenae*?[51] Perhaps, perhaps not.

Setting aside discussion of other strains which such proposals may put upon a philological decorum of interpretability, I want to interrogate them in terms of my code-based approach to toposness. Do the allusive reverberations just countenanced read as permutations within the fixed *topos*-code, or as extra-topical echoes of their predecessors *qua* 'modelli-esemplari'? The answer, I think, lies in between: these reverberations – conjectural reverberations, if you will – expose a mobility and renegotia-bility in the code of the 'many mouths' *topos* which is not usually acknowledged when such *topoi* are under description. When *Trist.* 1.5.53–6 and *Met.* 8.533–5 are read together, for instance, a common concern with the infinity of (funereal) woe emerges – a concern irrelevant to the archetype of the *topos* at *Il.* 2.488–90, but relevant again to a later 'many mouths' passage at Statius, *Theb.* 12.797–9. Can it not then be argued that the 'many mouths' *topos* has generated a subset-*topos* encoding, not just countlessness, but the countlessness *of woe*?

The fact is that conventional surveys of the *topos* leave unacknow-ledged many such constellations. What *does* the 'many mouths' *topos* encode? Simple (in)capacity to compass a huge theme or body of knowledge? (In)capacity to compass a huge theme or body of knowledge in the

---

[50] On Ovid's tendency to coopt motifs from his own earlier mythological poetry in constructing the 'myth' of his exile in *Trist.* and *Pont.*, see Hinds (1985), 26–7.

[51] Some years later, in *Pont.* 1.2.37–40, Ovid will compare the protracted *poena* of his exile to the punishment of Tityos, in language somewhat reminiscent of the Tityos vignette in Virgil's Tartarus (*Aen.* 6.595–600).

composition of epic poetry, and, if so, measured within epic itself in terms of what Homer could and could not do? or (as it seems from an Ovidian or Persian standpoint and also, perhaps, from the comic stand-points of Plautus and Caecilius[52]) in terms of what other genres can and cannot do *vis à vis* epic, Homeric or not?[53] To a Flavian the code might seem to be one of specifically *martial* countlessness – whose internal permutations would include the muster of forces in preparation for war (Valerius, *Arg.* 6.33–41; cf. *Il.* 2.488–90, thus reasserted as archetype), their slaughter in mid-war (Silius, *Pun.* 4.525–8), and their funerals (and the concomitant lamentations) at war's end (Statius, *Theb.* 12.797–9 again). Or yet another constellation (envisaged earlier in passing) might reconfigure the code as one of *didactic* countlessness (cf. *A.A.* 1.433–6, *Geo.* 2.43–4, Lucretius ap. Serv. *Geo.* 2.42). A move away from the *topos*-code may remain anomalous; but it will often have the potential to find incorporation as a subset or (more than that) as a rival configuration.

To return to a main concern of the chapter, the present section's accumulation of possibilities for the non-inert reading of a common-place adds its own challenge to the terms of a tidy 'philological contract' between author and reader. The ideal of a reader who sees exactly the same cues within the *topos* as the author, and constructs them in the same order and in the same way, will always in the final analysis be unattainable. This would not cease to be true even if we had access to the author's first readers (and to the most attentive and well-read among them). Nor, indeed, can the intervention of the author himself, i.e. the very first reader, be regarded as exempt from this ebb and flow of interpretative context.[54] Cues which on one reading are experienced as

---

[52] Plaut. *Bacch.* 128 (which rarely gets its billing as the earliest extant instance of the *topos* in Latin); Caecil. fr. 126–7 R.[3].

[53] To revisit the mathematics of the question, does the multiplication of mouths from 10 to 100 and beyond convey that epic subject-matter is now many times bigger than it was for Homer, or that the standard capacity of *one* mouth is now many times smaller than it was for Homer? The former implication is especially clear in Ov. *Trist.* 1.5 (see above), the latter in Ov. *Fast.* 2 (Homer's breast paired with 1,000 Ovidian [elegiac] voices) and in Sil. *Pun.* 4.525–8 (Homer's tongue paired with 100 Silian voices). For the latter implication I am indebted to Alessandro Barchiesi: in his words, 'il *topos* è frazionale e divisivo, non moltiplicativo e crescente'.

[54] A point to be reemphasized in chapter 5.

ABCDE will on another be experienced as AEBCD, on another as CGDBF – and so on. With *topoi*, and indeed with allusive discourse at large, one can never step into the same river twice.[55] No two readers will ever construct a set of cues in quite the same way; no one reader, even the author, will ever construct a set of cues in quite the same way twice. This is (almost) demonstrably true for our 'many mouths' *topos*, in which the ready availability of allusive markers, their proliferation and their slippage conspire simultaneously to invite and to frustrate interpretation; but it must even be true, in principle at least, for the most tightly-controlled and pointed system of allusion imaginable – even, say, for Catullus 64.1–18.

5   The limits of intertextualism

Most of the strategies adumbrated in the case-studies of sections 3 and 4 are indebted in some way to the semiological intertextualism which underpins Conte's approach to poetic imitation. The refusal to treat categories like 'confluence' or '*topos*' as inert or non-negotiable, the location of poet and readers in broader interpretative communities and in discursive contexts which problematize approaches predicated on precision, control and the tuning out of 'background noise' – these enlargements of philological debate are all energized by intertextualist inquiries whose scope can be as broad as discourse itself.[56]

Why not, then, abandon the apparatus of allusion altogether, and embrace intertextualism unconditionally?[57] As I argued towards the end of section 3, the term 'allusion' privileges the interventions in literary discourse of one intention-bearing subject, the alluding poet. But such an emphasis runs up against one of the most famous and broadly acknowledged impasses in twentieth century criticism: the ultimate

---

[55] – an image which might appropriately be used to deconstruct the idea of 'confluence'. R.G. Williams (1993), 51, offers a postmodern twist in a related context (cf. n.59 below): 'we cannot step into the same stream *once*' (emphasis mine).

[56] Genette (1982), 8–9; Conte (1986), 29n.11.

[57] When 'allusion' is renounced for 'intertextuality' (albeit not without qualms) by a critic who has worked as long and effectively with 'allusion' as has R.O.A.M. Lyne, it is clear that the question is now firmly on the poetic Latinist's agenda: see Lyne (1994).

unknowability of the poet's intention. Let us immediately concede the epistemological point, which is incontrovertible;[58] but let us not accept that as the end of the story.[59]

The intertextualist critic reacts to the *impasse* on the poet's intention by de-emphasizing the irretrievable moment of authorial production in favour of a more democratic stress upon plural moments of readerly consumption – on the grounds that, in practice, meaning is always constructed at the point of reception.[60] However, such an approach can shade into extremity. Just as there is a philological fundamentalism which occludes broader discursive dynamics in its privileging of tight authorial control (cf. section 1), so there is an opposite kind of fundamentalism – an intertextualist fundamentalism – which privileges readerly reception so single-mindedly as to wish the alluding author out of existence altogether. The useful heuristic metaphor of the 'death of the author'[61] has become too easy, and is too often justified through routine appeals to the liberation of the text from the supratextual speculations of (long-defunct) biographical intentionalists.[62] It is (or should be) much harder to justify the occlusion of the poet as a player in matters involving the close textual explication of particular phrases, lines or paragraphs.

Such an intertextualist fundamentalism, by treating the alluding author as an uninterpretable term, necessarily impoverishes our vocabulary for talking about many of the kinds of thing which I have tried to talk about in this chapter. The bracketing out of the author is often hailed as a liberation of meaning from the private into the public realm. Nevertheless, there is no getting away from the fact that the production

---

[58] *Pace* Knapp and Michaels (1982); my thanks to Tom Rosenmeyer for the reference, and for discussion of issues raised here and below.

[59] For a lively and finely nuanced treatment of intentionalism (which, almost despite itself, offers a vivid snapshot of the epistemological divisions which can make debate on this matter so difficult), see Frank Kermode *v* P.D. Juhl in Kermode (1983), 201–20. The issue has recently become pressing in the field of editorial theory: R.G. Williams (1993), esp. 55–64.

[60] Martindale (1993), 3–4 and *passim*; cf. Barthes (1989, cited in next n.), 54.

[61] As in Barthes (1989), an essay (first published in 1968) whose fine discriminations have not always registered in subsequent appropriations of the idea.

[62] A point made by Shawcross (1991), 1–13, who mobilizes some fine readings of 17th century poetry in defence of the relevance of a poet's intentions. However, in his revisionary account *relevance* slides too readily into *unproblematic knowability*.

of a poetic text *is* in some very important ways a private, self-reflexive, almost solipsistic activity; and even the poet's dialogue with the work of other poets can be a very private, self-reflexive and solipsistic kind of dialogue. These are truths sufficiently demonstrated in my own first chapter. The *resistance* which a reader encounters in the text because of that element of solipsism in the poet's production of the text is not, of course, the only kind of resistance which the reader faces in his or her intertextual negotiations. However, it is an important one, and the fact that it cannot in any individual instance be securely measured does not mean that it is not there, or that the readerly effort which it calls forth – the effort to connect – is any less real.

Recent modifications of intertextualist schemata, by Umberto Eco as well as by Conte, show that *some* interest in authorial subjectivity can be admitted by the back door into a text-and-reader-oriented intertextuality. The axiom that meaning is constructed at the point of reception becomes a better tool for dealing with the kinds of case which interest students of philological allusion if it embraces the fact (i.e. rather than occluding it) that one of the most persistent ways in which both Roman and modern readers construct the meaning of a poetic text is by attempting to construct from (and for) it an intention-bearing authorial voice, a construction which they generally hope or believe (in a belief which must always be partly misguided) to be a reconstruction; and the author thus (re)constructed is one who writes towards an implied reader who will attempt such a (re)construction.[63]

As a reader-oriented description of the contract between author and reader – a description which perhaps offers an *effect* of subjectivity as a stand-in for actual authorial subjectivity – the above sentence seems to me unimpeachable. However, there is no getting away from the fact that it involves a considerable amount of inefficient circumlocution. As a tool to think with, the rhetoric of intertextuality gets here into areas in which the rhetoric of allusivity, for all its own flaws and occlusions, just does better. Any theory of reader-constructed authorial intention, even the

---

[63] Cf. Eco's (1990), 58–9, idealizing description of the interaction of the 'model reader' with a 'model author', reiterated at Eco (1992), 64: 'Since the intention of the text is basically to produce a model reader able to make conjectures about it, the initiative of the model reader consists in figuring out a model author that is not the empirical one and that, in the end, coincides with the intention of the text'; also Conte (1994a), xviii-xx and (a fine discussion) 133–8.

best one, must remain intuitively resistant to the conceptualization and description of actual authorial initiative. Vocabularies of reader-oriented intertextuality, even when modified (as by Eco and Conte) to include 'textual intentions' associated with 'model authors', still manifest the intertextualist's inherent preference for the communal construction of meaning; such vocabularies can never be truly hospitable to the possibilities of tendentiousness, quirkiness or sheer surprise which add spice to the allusive practices of real authors.[64]

Therefore, while conceding the fact that, for us as critics, the alluding poet is ultimately and necessarily a figure whom we ourselves read out from the text, let us continue to employ our enlarged version of 'allusion', along with its intention-bearing author, as a discourse which is good to think with – which enables us to conceptualize and to handle certain kinds of intertextual transaction more economically and effectively than does any alternative.

A series of case-studies in allusive inexactitude, then, has yielded a poetic of corresponding inexactitude, which draws on but also distances itself from the rigidities of philological and intertextualist fundamentalisms alike. What my discussion has attempted to do is to blur those hard methodological edges by deploying a 'fuzzy logic' of allusive interpretability – to borrow a term from computer modelling which encodes precisely the paradox of exact inexactitude offered as a goal at the end of section 2.[65]

We shall not always choose in our day-to-day reading to pursue allusive reverberations as relentlessly as this chapter's case-studies have sought to do. That is fair enough, and as it should be: practical criticism has to make its compromises with practicable criticism; and there will always be readings in which (as in the readings of the Barthesian lover who lurks in my section 3 title) it will be more important to affirm the

---

[64] In my view, then, Conte's tendency to allow the author a little more presence in practice than he does in theory is a real *strength* (*pace* Conte (1994a), 178n.5; cf. section 1 *fin.* above): it is to this methodological 'impurity' that Conte's interpretations of Latin allusivity owe some of their distinct savour. Note Eco (1992), 67–88, a fascinating (and charming) attempt to negotiate the threshold between the claims of 'model author' and 'empirical author' – with the author of *The Name of the Rose* and *Foucault's Pendulum* as simultaneously 'guinea-pig and scientist'.

[65] 'Fuzzy logic' (the term was coined by Lotfi Zadeh) is a programming technology which enables computers to handle sets with imprecise membership criteria.

existence of a shared discourse than to classify the individual voices which make up that discourse.[66]

As philologists, we need not cease to offer tidy and controlled descriptions of allusions which poets themselves will often have tried to make tidy and controlled, provided that we do not confuse this aspiration to tidiness with an absoluteness of philological rigour. We need not cease to reify *topoi*, provided that we understand the provisionality of any such reification, for author and reader alike. We may even continue to use the deadpan 'cf.' when needed, provided that we treat it as an invitation to interpret rather than as the end of interpretation. The critic, like the poet, can bring only finite resources to the infinity of discourse.

[66] Cf. Barthes (1979), esp. 8–9.

Diachrony: literary history and its narratives

cedet Musa rudis ferocis Enni
(Statius, *Silvae* 2.7.75)

The unpolished Muse of savage Ennius shall give way to you

Statius wrote down the line, then scratched it out,
And scratched his head, and sat a while in doubt,
But wrote it down again a little later,
And said, 'Not bad, though, for a second-rater.'
(Louis MacKay)

The present chapter offers both an enlargement and a concomitant restriction of my theme: an enlargement, because I here offer some broader literary historical contexts within which to read the dynamics of allusive and intertextual appropriation; a restriction, because this broadening will be accompanied by an intensification of emphasis upon the *partiality* of any narrative told by any reader or writer about allusive or intertextual relations in literary history.

1 Importing the Muse

Claims of poetic primacy and innovation in Roman literary history down to the Augustan period are characteristically claims of an epiphany of Hellenic influence. Yet Roman literature is already thoroughly Hellenized from the earliest period of writing to which we have access. How often, and in what ways, can Greek literature come with the force of a revelation into a literary culture which is always already post-Hellenic?[1]

To focus the problem, consider Virgil's aspiration at the beginning of the third *Georgic* (3.10–12):

> primus ego in patriam mecum, modo vita supersit,
> Aonio rediens deducam vertice Musas;
> primus Idumaeas referam tibi, Mantua, palmas

> I shall be the first, returning from the Aonian peak, to draw down the Muses with me into my fatherland, provided life remain; I first, Mantua, shall bring you the palms of Idumaea . . .

Virgil, looking ahead to a future project of the highest ambition, evidently an epic, predicts that he will be the first to import the Greek Muses to Italy. But his claim is phrased in verses which clearly allude to a *previous* poet's claim to have been the first to import the Greek Muses to Italy – Ennius', invoked via the famous accolade offered by Lucretius early in *De Rerum Natura* (1.117–19),

> Ennius ut noster cecinit, qui primus amoeno
> detulit ex Helicone perenni fronde coronam
> per gentes Italas hominum quae clara clueret

> As our own Ennius sang, who first brought down from lovely Helicon a garland of perennial leafage to win a glorious name through the nations of Italian men

and probably directly too (cf. *Ann.* 208–10 Sk.; surviving fragments support the view that Lucretius describes Ennius in thoroughly Ennian terms):

> [cum] neque Musarum scopulos
> nec dicti studiosus [quisquam erat] ante hunc

> nos ausi reserare

> [When] no . . . the rough rocks of the Muses . . . nor [was anyone] studious of the word before this man . . . I dared unbar . . .

---

[1] This section has gained from dialogue with early versions of Feeney (1998), and with Alessandro Barchiesi's 'Passages to Italy: plots of Hellenization in Roman epic', with which it shared a platform at Leeds in May 1993; cf. also Greene (1982), 69–70 (on Hor. *Epist.* 1.19.19–34).

Ennius is flagged as the target of the Virgilian allusion by an even clearer reference in the immediately preceding line:

> . . . temptanda via est, qua me quoque possim
> tollere humo *victorque virum volitare per ora*   (*Geo.* 3.8–9)

I too must try a path, whereby I may raise myself from the ground and fly victorious on the lips of men

> nemo me lacrimis decoret nec funera fletu
> faxit. cur? *volito vivos per ora virum*   (Enn. *min.* 46 Courtney)

Let none adorn me with tears, or make a funeral with wailing. Why? I fly alive on the lips of men.

In a very Roman paradox, then, Virgil's claim to be first is 'authorized' by its association with Ennius' claim to be first – even though the Ennian precedent can be argued precisely to disqualify the Virgilian claim. What kind of cultural reprocessing has taken place to allow Virgil's claim to stand?

We should not allow this paradox to be diluted by special pleading (as of course it can be), whether absurd or reasonable. An absurd attempt to reconcile the two claims would argue that in the Virgil *primus* = *primus Mantuanorum* ('first among Mantuans').[2] A reasonable attempt to reconcile the claims would say that *primus . . . deducam* (*Geo.* 3.10–11) can coexist with *primus . . . detulit* (Lucr. 1.117–18) because it makes a more specific claim: Ennius (as reported by Lucretius) simply 'brings down' the Muses' garland; Virgil 'brings down' the Muses 'in a specifically Callimachean manner', brings them down (through the Augustan poets' favourite buzz-word) in a *carmen deductum*, a fine-drawn song; and, in line with this, he varies 'Helicon' with the more recherché 'Aonian peak', using an adjective first attested in Callimachus. A reasonable counter to this reasonable reconciliation would point out that Virgil's *deducam* also functions as an image of leading back in military triumph (an implication promoted by the reference to palms in the following line) – so that the usurpation of Ennius again becomes stark. Who would more properly speak of being

---

[2] . . . *non Romanorum, quod superbum esset* ' . . . not among Romans, which would be arrogance' (P. Wagner), quoted and dismissed by Thomas (1988a) ad *Geo.* 3.11; see Thomas too for the 'Callimachean' approach.

the first to bring the Muses bodily to Italy in a context of military campaigning? Why, Ennius, of course, in his famous association with his patron and general M. Fulvius Nobilior, importer from Ambracia as spoils of war of a set of Greek Muse-statues for a new shrine and cult of 'Hercules of the Muses' in Rome (more on this below) – which is also the counter to the further plea that Virgil promises to bring back the Muses themselves whereas Ennius had brought back only a garland from the home of the Muses.

Back, therefore, to the initial paradox. If Virgil says 'I shall be the first to bring the Muses to Italy' and in doing so alludes to a famous statement that 'Ennius was the first to bring the Muses to Italy', at a literal level his allusion exposes his claim as a lie. At a more complex level it tells us something about how Hellenizing revolutions often operate in Roman poetry and in Roman literary historical self-fashioning in the last centuries BCE: they operate through a revision of previous Hellenizing revolutions, a revision which can be simultaneously an appropriation and a denial.[3]

In a sense, what *Geo.* 3.10–11 does is not so much proclaim a beginning for Virgil as proclaim the end of Ennius. To generalize the lesson, proclamations of one poet's newness are inevitably proclamations of another poet's oldness. We may take our bearings here from a very simple but often neglected truth: archaic poets are never aware of the fact that they are archaic poets. An 'archaic period' is always something invented by later poets or critics. Therefore, in studying poets commonly deemed to be 'archaic' it is important not to leave that term uninterrogated. To construct a poet as 'archaic' is necessarily to be complicit with a history of reception; and modern literary historians should never adopt that label for a given poet without examining its history, and testing the limits of their own complicity with that history.

It is not that we should deny to the ancient poets under discussion here the right to carve out cultural space for themselves by consigning their predecessors to the dustbin, or the archive room, of literary history. What we should worry about is how unreflectively we modern literary historians sometimes repeat their moves, without having the excuse they had of needing old Roman poets to define their own Roman poetic newness. Especially in the case of early writers who have come down to

---

[3] With the foregoing cf. esp. Hardie (1993), 100–1.

us only in fragments and stripped of many of their original contexts, we are often too ready to define them in the terms in which their more canonical successors defined them, without attempting to put some space between those interested evaluations and ours. (Not that our own evaluations can ultimately avoid being implicated in the discourses of taste and canonicity which we inherit from antiquity – a point to which I shall return.)

We have seen how Virgil reads Ennius' importation of the Greek Muses to Italy. Let us now look at fragment 1 Sk. of the *Annales*, and instead of reading it, like Augustans, as 'old poetry', let us attempt to resist the later history of its reception and to read it as 'new poetry'.

> Musae quae pedibus magnum pulsatis Olympum

> Muses, who with your feet beat mighty Olympus . . .

The terms of such a reading are in fact familiar enough (Ennius has his modern apologists); and, naturally, this narrative of poetic innovation is the narrative of an epiphany of Greek influence.

The opening word of address in fragment 1 (the *incipit* of the epic, or at least the most emphatic word in an opening period[4]) immediately proclaims a Hellenizing innovation: *Musae*. Thus Skutsch ad loc.: 'The poet invokes the Muses instead of the *Camenae*, to whom Livius Andronicus in his translation of the *Odyssey* and apparently Naevius in the *Carmen Belli Punici* had addressed themselves. He thus expresses his intention to subject Roman poetry more closely to the discipline of Greek poetic form.' An epiphany of Hellenizing innovation, then, concentrated in one word. And the line contains a further proclamation of newness: its very shape, its very movement, proclaims a new wave of Hellenic influence. This is not the metre used by Livius Andronicus and Naevius, not the saturnian, but something new for Latin epic: the dactylic hexameter. A final observation may be added. Invocations of poetic goddesses do not invariably focus upon their dancing feet; this invocation does, not because of some robust archaic association of poetry with vigorous stamping in the dance,[5] nor even (primarily) to

---

[4] For the latter (minority) position cf. Skutsch (1985) ad loc.

[5] I.e. as an Augustan might read the line – on the analogy of Hor. *Carm.* 3.18.15–16 or Ov. *A.A.* 1.111–12 (with the suggestive n. of Hollis (1977) ad loc.).

signal a debt to Hesiod (*Theog.* 1–8, 68–71), but to 'annotate' through a reflexive pun in the word *pes* the metrical innovation which is being enacted even as we read.[6]

A modern proem presents itself, then, not an archaic one. How selfish Virgil's eclipse of this exciting moment now seems, viewed from a second-century vantage point. But our act of recuperation has only pushed the problem of literary historical partiality one step back, not escaped it. We have saved Ennius from Virgil in *Ann.* 1 Sk. so as to redeem him as a new poet; but Ennius is no more generous to the generations of Hellenizing poets who precede him in Latin than was Virgil to Ennius himself. Ennius' 'modern' proem entails the 'creation' of two archaic poets: Livius Andronicus and Naevius.

This becomes clearer in the fragments of the Book 7 proem (some of them already cited), in which Ennius offers a famous disparagement of the saturnian poetry of his Roman predecessors,[7] and specifically of the *Bellum Punicum* of Naevius, in a 'proemio al mezzo' within the *Annales* (206–10 Sk.):[8]

> scripsere alii rem
> vorsibus quos olim Fauni vatesque canebant
>
> [cum] neque Musarum scopulos
> nec dicti studiosus [quisquam erat] ante hunc
>
> nos ausi reserare
>
> Others have written of the matter in verses which once the Fauns and seers used to sing . . . (etc.)

In section 2 we shall find no less a commentator than Cicero (*Brut.* 75–6) chiding Ennius for his lack of generosity here in acknowledging how much his epic owes to the 'Faun'-like Naevius. For now the effects of such ungenerousness on an earlier predecessor merit consideration.

Is Ennius the first poet to import the Greek Muses to Italy? For

---

[6] An 'annotation' all the more pointed (Alessandro Barchiesi suggests to me) 'because the *Saturnius*, of all lines, is the one which has no *pedes* at all'.

[7] For *Ann.* 207 as a designation of saturnian verse see the *testimonium* at Varr. *L.L.* 7.36.

[8] Ennius' 'proem in the middle': Conte (1984), 128–9.

economy's sake I pass over the dispute as to whether Naevius may conceivably have named the Muses as such too.[9] Rather, I go back to the poet who stands at the very beginning of the Roman epic tradition: Livius Andronicus, translator into Latin saturnians of Homer's *Odyssey*. In *Ann.* 208–9 Livius is implicitly subject to the same dismissal as a primitive as is Naevius, to whom *Ann.* 206–7 refer.[10] He too is not *dicti studiosus*; he too has never scaled the *Musarum scopulos*.

But Livius in his turn deserves a chance to be read as a new poet, even if it is his fate always to be constructed as the old, archaic poet, the 'predecessor' of Ennius. Let me now try to recapture the modernity of *his* epic proem, something which critics in our time have found harder to do than they have with Ennius, perhaps because (unlike in Ennius' case, as we shall see later) there is no extant ancient paradigm for such a reading:

> virum mihi, Camena,   insece versutum   (Liv. Andr. *Odusia* fr. 1)

> ἄνδρα μοι ἔννεπε, Μοῦσα, πολύτροπον . . .   (Homer, *Od.* 1.1)

Tell me, [Goddess of song], of the man of many turns . . .

In an Enniocentric history of early Latin poetry, *Camena*, one of the ancient Italian water divinities identified with a spring outside Rome's

---

[9] The evidence for Naevius' employment of *Camenae* rather than *Musae* is highly equivocal, and the terms of the modern argument are more heavily dictated by Ennius' tendentious characterization of Naevius as a primitive than is usually acknowledged. One cause of uncertainty is that key ancient *testimonia* in the dispute are not 'about' the *Camena v Musa* question at all, and hence may use the name which they use in an unmarked way. Thus *Musa* at Porcius Licinus fr. 1 (taking it as referring to Naevius and drawing out implications from Courtney (1993) ad loc.) is probably a metonymy for 'poetry' *tout court* and a red herring in the *Camena v Musa* question. For Naevian *Camenae* see (again with Courtney) the (non-Naevian) 'Epitaph' of Naevius 1–2: *immortales mortales si foret fas flere, / flerent divae Camenae Naevium poetam* 'if it were lawful for gods to cry for mortals, the divine Camenae would cry for the poet Naevius', where *Camenae can* probably be trusted as a marked specification, since what is at issue in the ensuing conceit (3–4) is a collective forgetting of the Latin language at Rome after Naevius' death; cf. Courtney's tentative gloss: 'because of the influence of Ennius a Hellenizing tendency has now taken over'. *Some* degree of equivocation is built into Naevius' usage, even if he does (as most believe) favour *Camenae*: see n.14 below.

[10] Cicero's *testimonium* in the *Brutus* makes the disparaging reference to Livius explicit (*Brut.* 71, quoted in section 2 below). I follow Skutsch's (1985) likely restoration ad loc. of the Ennian sequence of thought from Cicero's appropriative excerpting.

Porta Capena, represents the old habit with which Ennius broke. Indeed Ennius seems to have built into the proem of *Annales* 10 a specific 'correction' of the Livian *incipit*, taking over Livius' distinctive verb *insece* (of which more in a moment) but 'correcting' *Camena* to *Musa* (*Ann.* 322–3 Sk.):

> *insece Musa* manu Romanorum induperator
> quod quisque in bello gessit cum rege Philippo

> Tell, Muse, what each Roman commander wrought by force in the war with King Philip.

Another fragment, though dogged by modern controversy, may even show Ennius explicitly negotiating the transition from *Camena* to *Musa*, possibly in the context of an account in Book 15 of the dedication of Fulvius' (already mentioned) *templum Herculis Musarum* (*Ann.* 487 [*sed. incert.*] Sk.):[11]

> Musas quas memorant nosces nos esse Camenas

> You will learn that we *Camenae* are those whom they call *Musae* . . .

Whether or not they entertain this last piece of evidence, modern literary historians have been almost unanimous in reading Ennius' 'advance' in the matter of poetry-goddesses in strictly Ennian terms.[12] To repeat the earlier quotation from Skutsch, by invoking the Muses instead of the *Camenae*, Ennius 'expresses his intention to subject Roman poetry more closely to the discipline of Greek poetic form'. The implication is that Livius' rendering of Homer's Μοῦσα as *Camena* shows him to be a less disciplined Hellenizer (not *dicti studiosus*, as it were). So too Ernout-Meillet s.v. *Camenae* (my translation): 'The old Latin poets, Livius Andronicus and Naevius, used the name *Camenae* to replace "the Muses"; it was a crude/crass equivalent (Fr. *grossière*) and Ennius, followed by his successors, simply transcribed the Greek "*Musae*".'

---

[11] Everything about this fragment has been contested: attribution, placement, metre, reconstruction and emendation, interpretation (cf. esp. Suerbaum (1968), 347–9 with bibl.). For *nosce* I read Jordan's metre-regularizing *nosces*, commended but not adopted by Skutsch.

[12] Dissenters are led by Mariotti (1986, 1st ed. 1952), esp. 26 'la sua linea direttiva fu *diversa* da quella di Ennio' (my emph.); cf. also G. Williams and A.S. Gratwick in *CHCL* 2.58 and 79–80.

Ennius emerges from such analyses endowed with a combination of learnedness and restraint which gives his programme an anachronistically neoteric ring.

But why should this be the obvious way to read the two choices? Is it really self-evident that it marks an *advance* in Hellenizing innovation to transliterate a Greek goddess into the Roman alphabet rather than to seek an Italian cultural analogue to render her in her new context? Descriptions of Ennius' innovation in the matter of the poetry-goddess sometimes come oddly close to forgetting to acknowledge that a Μοῦσα lay behind Livius' *Camena* at all. Here is H.D. Jocelyn's version of the Enniocentric narrative: 'Instead of invoking the old Italian *Camenae* as had been done by Livius in his translation of the *Odyssey* and by Naevius in his *Carmen Belli Punici*, [Ennius] addressed himself to the Μοῦσαι, goddesses who first became known to speakers of Latin when Fulvius began building in the Campus Martius . . . a temple for *Hercules Musarum* with the proceeds of his Aetolian campaign.'[13] In the face of the confident progressivist rhetoric of a sentence like this, it takes a real effort to hold on to the underlying fact that there was at least one important speaker of Latin who knew of one Greek Μοῦσα, Homer's, long before Fulvius laid his first foundation: Livius Andronicus. Livius quite evidently chose to invoke the *Camena* not out of some twilit ignorance of the Muse, but out of a different view of how the Muse should be translated from Greece to Rome.[14]

If he had lived long enough to see what Ennius made of his feat of translation, what would Livius have thought? I do not think it wholly facetious to suggest that he might have seen Ennius' *Musa* as a retrograde step, a cruder alternative to his own strategy. From his own partial viewpoint as a self-conscious translator, Livius might well have rejected the transliterated Muse, and continued to favour the indigenous water-

---

[13] Jocelyn (1972), 997–8.

[14] That Livius' *Camena* asks to be read with the Muse *sous rature* is also evident from fr. 21 Bü, which refers to her as the daughter of *Moneta*, evidently a mother adopted as an etymological analogue to the Muses' mother Mnemosyne. Such negotiation between traditions may illuminate the case of Naevius too (cf. n.9): if Livius could give his *Camena* a Roman version of Mnemosyne as mother, Naevius (fr. 1 Bü) could refer to his goddesses, even with allusion to Hesiod, *Theog.* 60 and 76 (so Mariotti (1955), 53–6), as *novem Iovis concordes filiae sorores* 'nine harmonious sisters, daughters of Jove', without that entailing an abandonment of the name *Camenae*.

divinity of his *Odusia* proem, with its etymologizing suggestiveness (*Casmena/Carmena–carmen*),[15] as offering a more energetic and thought-ful Romanization of the alien poetry-goddesses of the Hippocrene.

I describe Livius as a translator self-conscious about his art. Even if we look no further than this opening line of his *Odusia*, there is more than the *Camena* here to bear witness to this. The verb *insece* has rightly attracted notice. In Sander Goldberg's recent account (but the point goes back to Mariotti), 'with *insece* [Livius] offers a rare Latin word of similar meaning, sound and accent to Homer's own uncommon ἔννεπε'. If Livius was etymologizing, it happens that he was spot on;[16] equally interesting is the point about the rarity of the word, probably an archa-ism *even for Livius*, bearing witness as it does to his detailed sophistica-tion as a translator.[17]

A final suggestion may help to promote a narrative for Livius' epic proem independent of Ennian teleology. If we are prepared to allow to his *incipit*-line the concentratedness of meaning commonly granted to an *incipit* in 'new poetry', we may just see his artistic self-consciousness further demonstrated in a deft programmatic pun through which he defines his project and differentiates it from Homer's.[18] 'Tell me, *Camena*, of the man who is *versutus*.' *Versutus*: 'characterized by turns', like the Greek πολύτροπος; but in particular characterized by the 'turn' which he has undergone from the Greek language into the Latin. *Vertere* is the technical term *par excellence* for 'translation' in early Latin literature (as in *Plautus vortit barbare*);[19] and here in this programmatically loaded context our poet introduces a Ulysses in whom the very linguistic switch to which he owes his textual existence has been made part of his proverbial versatility, has been troped into

---

[15] See Varr. *L.L.* 7.26–7; Maltby (1991) s.v. *Camena*. The probability that the Muse-*Camena* link originates with Livius himself is high: see Waszink (1979), incl. the suggestion that Livius was influenced in his choice by a (prior?) association of the *Camenae* with prophecy.

[16] Ernout-Meillet (1959) s.v. **insequo*. More details in n.37 below.

[17] So Mariotti (1986), 28; cf. Goldberg (1995), 64. More elaborate claims may go too far: so Kearns (1990).

[18] With the following point cf. Suerbaum (1968), 9–10, on the identity of the authorial self inscribed in Livius' *mihi* (*vis à vis* Homer's μοι). The fear of retrofitting Livius with too much poetic sophistication dogs many modern discussions; it can usefully be counter-balanced by a fear of underestimating him.

[19] Cf. *OLD* 'verto' 24; Plaut. *Trin.* 19 'Plautus turned it into a foreign tongue'.

his πολυτροπία.[20] What hero could more aptly be celebrated by the artfully translated Muse of *Odusia* fr.1?

These latest pages have considered two different ways to import the Muses to Rome: some may prefer Ennius' solution, some Livius'. Some, indeed, may prefer the kind of Muse-translation offered by Ennius' patron Fulvius Nobilior, who, not content merely to scan the cultural, linguistic or alphabetical codes on paper, makes *his* translation concrete by hauling the Muses bodily across the Ionian Sea and housing them in a temple on the Campus Martius. Fulvius (who may be suspected from other evidence too of serious interest in *res divinae*) was himself 'no boorish *gloriosus*':[21] we should not underestimate the subtlety of the negotiations between Muse and *Camena* implied by his interventions in the field of public works. The sources suggest that the general who transformed an existing temple of Hercules the Great Guardian by housing in it his imported statues of the Muses also moved thither a small monument to the *Camenae* attributed to Numa, which had lacked a permanent home since being moved from its original location beyond the Porta Capena (where it had been struck by a lightning bolt).[22] The cultural and religious negotiations involved in these manoeuvres are complex, and it should be evident that they are just as much in need of properly dynamic and wary construal as are the moves made in the poetic texts.[23] In particular, although (as E. Badian has well argued) the Ennian narrative in some sense dramatizes the Fulvian one and is thus heavily complicit with it, the inevitability of differences between the two should also be respected: each version of the story, the politician's and

---

[20] Denis Feeney and Jim Porter suggest to me that Livius' reflexive annotation (if such it is) should be put into dialogue with ancient debate concerning the interpretation of Ulysses' 'original' epithet πολύτροπος: cf. esp. the interpretation of the epithet in the sense 'of many turns of language' attributed in the scholia (ad 1.1) to Antisthenes, and provocatively explored by Pucci (1982), 50–7.

[21] Quotation from Goldberg (1995), 130–1, who sets out the evidence for Fulvius' interest in antiquarian research.

[22] On Fulvius' temple of *Hercules Musarum*, built with the proceeds of his Aetolian campaign (either shortly after his return to Rome in 187 BCE or during his censorship of 179), see Cic. *Arch.* 27, Plin. *Nat.* 35.66, Eumen. *Paneg. Lat.* 9.7.3; on the transfer to it of the Numan shrine of the *Camenae* see Serv. on *Aen.* 1.8.

[23] Especially wary, in that key *testimonia* (distinctions of nomenclature not being the point at issue for them; cf. n.9 above) vertiginously confuse the names in a way which perhaps does not sufficiently embarrass modern historians: Eumenius actually bears witness to Ambracian *Camenae*, and Servius to Numan *Musae*!

the epic poet's, will have had 'its own rationale and its own integrity'.[24] The story of the importation of the Muse is a story told in different ways by different voices; it is a story involving elements of domestication, usurpation, syncretism and continuing dialogue, which may not admit of being resolved into a single linear narrative.

With Fulvius' role duly acknowledged, the particular lessons of my reading of the Livian proem may be restated. First, neither Ennius nor Fulvius is importing something *de novo*; both are extending and appropriating a narrative of importation which is already in play in *Odusia* fr. 1. Second, for a modern critic to read Livius' importation of the Muse as inherently more primitive than Ennius', to regard the latter as self-evidently an advance in Hellenization, may be to internalize too unconditionally an Enniocentric view of literary history.

One formulation towards which this case-study has been working – involving a 'strong' or deliberately overstated proposition[25] – is this: are Hellenizing revolutions such as Livius Andronicus / Ennius / Virgil to be seen unreservedly as a progressive series of steps (e.g. progressing towards an Augustan *telos*); or is there a sense in which they should be read as recurrent but essentially static renegotiations of the same cultural move?

The more moderate or 'weaker' version of this proposition would be that all the ancient literary historical viewpoints which we inherit are partial and tendentious, all involve the imposition of some kind of teleology; so that if we as modern critics privilege one of these viewpoints to the exclusion of another, we had better be aware of what we are doing.

2 Old poets

Let me now follow up the discussion in section 1 by multiplying the viewpoints from which the literary historical placement of Ennius and his predecessors may be contemplated. Section 2 will look at three ancient treatments of early Roman epic from three different vantage points in three different periods, each of which is overtly concerned with questions of progress and obsolescence: Cicero, *Brutus* 71–6; Horace, *Epist.*

[24] A valuable emphasis at Goldberg (1995), 131; cf. Badian (1972), 187–95.
[25] For this way of framing an argument cf. Martindale (1993), 7.

2.1.50–75; and Gellius, *Noct. Att.* 12.2. Both individually and in combination, these commentaries will highlight some of the issues involved in the construction of archaic poetry: in their teleologies and partialities, in what they show of shifts in taste and in perspective over time and between different readers of the same time, they may help to illustrate the hazards for the modern critic of buying into one version of literary history to the exclusion of others – a lesson to be brought front and centre for an especially privileged set of 'new poets' in section 3. My survey will also serve to reveal the surprising persistence of Ennius' *Annales* 7 proem as a nexus for Roman critical thinking about these issues.

It is to my first passage, in fact, in Cicero's *Brutus* (46 BCE), that we owe our fullest glimpse of the moment in the middle of the *Annales* in which Ennius makes Naevius into an archaic poet. Cicero's reading of the relationship between the two is essentially in line with Ennius' own, and anticipates the modern Enniocentric orthodoxy (on which it has undoubtedly been a formative influence). However, while not disrupting this Ennian teleology Cicero is concerned to offer a kinder, gentler version of it – and, indeed, to suggest that Ennius himself may subscribe to his version.[26]

Cicero's interest may be declared at once: his comments on early Latin poetry are made to illustrate an argument, not about poetry, but about one of its sister arts. The *Brutus*, we should bear in mind, is a diachronic and teleological history of *oratory* – just where its *telos* is positioned is a matter on which, like Cicero, I shall suspend comment at this stage – and in the larger context of our passage Cicero, as lead speaker in his dialogue, is concerned with the neglect of Cato by modern orators. Roman oratory alone among the arts (he argues in sections 69ff.) lacks a vocabulary to praise the archaic stages of an art which has since attained perfection. In sculpture (in contrast), we admire the perfection of Polyclitus but, recognizing that this perfection is not achieved without a process of development, we acknowledge the importance of giving due honour to his predecessors. Cicero offers in 70 a narrative of development from the statues of Canachus, 'too stiff to reproduce the truth of

---

[26] Goldberg (1995), 5–12, published after this section was drafted, anticipates me in using the *Brutus* to explore the construction of Roman literary history. His account of Cicero's teleological scheme is more spacious, mine more detailed; methodologically our treatments offer a mixture of complementarity and contrast. Cf. (still) M. Barchiesi (1962), 21–38, for its many fine touches.

nature' (*rigidiora . . . quam ut imitentur veritatem*), to those of Calamis, 'still hard, and yet softer than those of Canachus' (*dura illa quidem, sed tamen molliora quam Canachi*), to those of Myron, 'not yet fully natural, though one would not hesitate to call them beautiful' (*nondum . . . satis ad veritatem adducta, iam tamen quae non dubites pulchra dicere*). Only after being thus praised does Myron yield in turn to Polyclitus, whose statues are 'still more beautiful and indeed in my estimation quite perfect' (*pulchriora etiam Polycliti et iam plane perfecta, ut mihi quidem videri solent*). At this point, rather than rounding off the sculptural comparison by explicitly drawing the conclusion (i.e. Cato's oratory, rather than being ignored, should be admired as an important milestone on the path to perfection), Cicero proceeds instead to elaborate his analogy from the other arts, referring especially and most emphatically to poetry. Hence his kind words for a 'Myron-like' Naevius – within an account which, however, is just as sure as is Ennius' own that Naevius is a stage *en route* to an Ennian *telos* (75–6):

> tamen illius, quem in vatibus et Faunis annumerat Ennius, bellum Punicum quasi Myronis opus delectat. sit Ennius sane, ut est certe, perfectior: qui si illum, ut simulat, contemneret, non omnia bella persequens primum illud Punicum acerrimum bellum reliquisset. sed ipse dicit cur id faciat: 'scripsere', inquit, 'alii rem vorsibus' – et luculente quidem scripserunt, etiam si minus quam tu polite; nec vero tibi aliter videri debet, qui a Naevio vel sumpsisti multa, si fateris, vel, si negas, surripuisti

> For all that Ennius counts Naevius among the 'seers and Fauns', his *Bellum Punicum*, like a work of Myron, still gives pleasure. Let Ennius be, as he assuredly is, more perfect in execution: yet if he really despised Naevius, as he professes, he would not in undertaking to describe all our wars have left out that sharply contested first Punic War. But he tells us himself why he does so: 'Others', he says, 'have written of the matter in verses' – yes, and splendidly too they wrote, even if with less polish than you, sir; and you ought not indeed to think otherwise, since there is much from Naevius that you have either taken over, if you confess the debt, or stolen, if you deny it.

What Cicero offers, then, is a notably less confrontational version of Ennius' own statement of his relationship to Naevius – a version which he seeks, despite Ennius, to reconcile with the Ennian version, arguing that the later poet's polemic itself entails an act of homage.[27] The passage is worth savouring as one of the few overt analyses of allusion in Roman rhetorical or critical prose to approach the subtlety of the poets' own exercises in theory-in-practice.

If Naevius corresponds to Myron in *Brut.* 75–6, on Cicero's analysis, then Ennius is clearly implied to be a Polyclitus. Yet (to sneak a relativizing glance ahead in time) the very qualities for which Ennius is praised in Cicero's account, polish and high finish, are those which his poetry will famously lack in the eyes of Augustan poets for whom that same Ennius will be the proverbial archaic poet: *Ennius arte carens* ('lacking in art', Ov. *Am.* 1.15.19); Ennius of the shaggy crown (Prop. 4.1.61 *hirsuta . . . corona*)[28] and shaggy *Annales* (Ov. *Trist.* 2.259 *nihil est hirsutius illis*). A problem looms here. If 'nothing is more hirsute than the *Annales*', as Ovid claims, how is one from such a viewpoint to read Naevius *vis à vis* Ennius? That question is no concern of Ovid's in the *Tristia* passage just cited; but, as we shall see below, precisely such a question is raised in another Augustan discussion, in Horace's second book of *Epistles*.

The difference in perspective between Cicero and the Augustans is most easily explicable in terms of the passage of time and of literary fashion; it is probably significant that those Propertian and Ovidian characterizations of the *Annales* belong to the years in which the *Aeneid* is establishing itself as the new standard of Roman epic. However, even a narrative as plausible as this may flatten the topography of literary history. As I hinted at the outset, there is an element of caginess in Cicero's diachronic account of Roman oratory in the *Brutus*; and a brief excursus on this may reveal the Ciceronian designation of Ennius as the culmination of the artistic development of Latin poetry to be complicated by a personal and somewhat disingenuous teleology of Cicero's own.

Briefly, the account given by Cicero describes oratory as reaching perfection a full generation before himself, with Marcus Antonius and L.

---

[27] The tone of the *Ann.* 7 proem evidently fascinated Cicero: cf. *Orat.* 171 (with 169) where he invokes its precedent in claiming the privilege to criticize the ancients, while carefully pointing out the greater conditionality, and lesser egotism, of his own criticism.

[28] This connects with Prop. 3.1.15–20 and (hence) alludes to Ennius' *perenni fronde coronam* at Lucr. 1.118, discussed in section 1: Miller (1983), 283–7.

Licinius Crassus[29] (the orators whom he had cast as the leading inter-
locutors in *De Oratore* nine years previously). Despite the good reasons
offered for regarding the careers of these two as marking a point of
culmination,[30] a student of Ciceronian self-advertisement may sense an
unspoken supplement; and, sure enough, shortly before the end of the
Brutus Cicero has one of the interlocutors, Atticus, call his professed
telos into question. Atticus accuses Cicero (the participant) of disingenu-
ous modesty *vis à vis* himself in his overly lavish praise of early Roman
orators, starting with Cato (293 'an excellent and remarkable man – no
one shall say otherwise – but an orator?'); he concludes by looking
askance at Cicero's enthusiasm for Antonius and Crassus, and in par-
ticular at the deferential treatment given to one particular Crassan
speech (296):[31]

> venio ad eos in quibus iam perfectam putas esse eloquentiam, quos
> ego audivi, sine controversia magnos oratores, Crassum et Anto-
> nium. de horum laudibus tibi prorsus assentior, sed tamen non isto
> modo: ut Polycliti Doryphorum sibi Lysippus aiebat, sic tu
> suasionem legis Serviliae tibi magistram fuisse. haec germana ironia
> est. cur ita sentiam non dicam, ne me tibi assentari putes

> I come to those in whom you consider that perfect eloquence was
> finally realized, Crassus and Antonius, indisputably great orators
> both; I myself heard them speak. With your praise of them I am
> heartily in agreement, and yet not quite as you put it: you said that the
> speech of Crassus in support of the *lex Servilia* was your teacher – in
> the same manner I suppose as Lysippus used to say that the
> Doryphorus of Polyclitus was his model. Your pose here is pure
> Socratic irony. Why I think so I shall not say lest you suspect me of
> flattery.

[29] See esp. *Brut.* 143 *equidem quamquam Antonio tantum tribuo . . . , tamen Crasso nihil
statuo fieri potuisse perfectius* 'though I assign so much to Antonius . . . , yet I hold
that nothing could have been more perfect than Crassus'.

[30] A culmination which the reader of *De Oratore* (esp. 3.1–12) will also remember as
an eve of catastrophe.

[31] Cicero (the participant) had in fact left the door open just a crack for an interven-
tion of this kind: cf. his words on the Servilian speech at 161, *iam ad summum paene
esse perductam* 'now brought to all but the highest finish', and the coy exchange
with Brutus prompted by this qualification – in contrast to his earlier definitive
statement (143), quoted in n.29 above.

What catches the eye here, in the context of our discussion, is the fate of the Ciceronian vocabulary of analogy explored back in sections 69ff. in connexion with Cato. The moment of Polyclitan perfection towards which Roman oratory was headed, on Cicero's narrative, is identified in this passage with Crassus' speech on the *lex Servilia*; but Atticus' 'heterodox' reading appropriates and disrupts that teleology by casting Cicero himself as a Lysippus who renders the Polyclitan form of perfection obsolete.[32] This Attican reading (if we may play along with Cicero in calling it that) has the potential to reverberate elsewhere in the system of analogy deployed in 69ff. If Cicero has a vested interest in the *Brutus* in defining a form of perfection which is (in effect) open to transcendence, should the moments of perfection adduced for the other arts perhaps be read as susceptible of transcendence too? Sculpture is perfected in Polyclitus, Roman oratory in Crassus – but only until Cicero has Atticus reconfigure those teleologies. What, then, of Ennius? A suspicious reading might now be tempted to probe Cicero's praise of Ennian polish and high finish[33] – and to wonder just where Cicero (no mean hexameter stylist himself) might look in his own time to see *that* form of perfection transcended. This may be over-elaborate; but my excursus serves to dramatize the point that Cicero's commentary on early Roman epic is a tendentious one, with a very particular agenda to serve.

Earlier in his comments on Ennius' *Annales* 7 proem Cicero, less committed to rescuing Livius Andronicus than Naevius from Ennian triumphalism, reaches back beyond Myron, back even beyond Calamis and Canachus, to find his sculptural analogy for this first pioneer of Latin epic (71):

'. . . nec dicti studiosus' quisquam erat 'ante hunc', ait ipse de se, nec mentitur in gloriando: sic enim sese res habet. nam et Odyssia Latina est sic tamquam opus aliquod Daedali et Livianae fabulae non satis dignae quae iterum legantur

---

[32] On Lysippus, cf. Stewart (1990), 186, with Plin. *Nat.* 34.65 *vulgoque dicebat ab illis factos quales essent homines, a se quales viderentur esse* 'he used commonly to say that whereas his predecessors had made men as they were, he made them as they appeared to be'; also *Nat.* 34.61 for the anecdote that Lysippus was inspired to take up sculpture by the dictum of the painter Eupompus that 'it was Nature herself, not an artist, whom one should imitate'.

[33] In another (famous) context, commenting on a stylistic preference among *poetae novi*, Cicero does very precisely relativize Ennian polish: *Orat.* 161.

' . . . nor' was anyone 'studious of the word before this man', as says our poet of himself; nor is he false in his boast. It is just so, for the Latin *Odyssey* is as it were a statue of Daedalus, and the plays of Livius do not merit a second reading.

Cicero is clearly not in the business of handing out compliments here; yet, given the customarily numinous associations of 'Daedalic' statuary, his analogy for Livius' *Odusia* may carry just a fleeting implication of reverence or awe for the antique artefact despite its lack of even a Canachan degree of finish.[34] In that case the closest parallel would be Quintilian's judgement well over a century later, not on Livius, but on Ennius himself, as being like an ancient grove whose great old oaks offer more sanctity than beauty (*Inst.* 10.1.88; cf. chapter 1, section 3 above): *Ennium sicut sacros vetustate lucos adoremus, in quibus grandia et antiqua robora iam non tantam habent speciem quantam religionem.* Quintilian's reverence here might have been just as galling for Ennius, had he been endowed with foresight, as any Augustan irreverence about 'hirsute' epics. In either case the lesson is the same. Once a new poet becomes an old poet, his revolution can disappear from view as his work is assimilated – by admirers and detractors alike – to an undifferentiated, 'levelled' category of old poetry.

Nowhere is this phenomenon more succinctly observed than in my second commentary, from Horace's *Epistle to Augustus*, a difficult passage most recently interpreted by Peter White.[35] The Horatian lines bear witness that just such an assimilation of Ennius to his predecessors has become the norm among Augustan readers, in their undifferentiated and uncritical admiration for all archaic poetry; Horace himself (on White's reading adding a subtle discrimination to his own polemic against the dominance of the archaic) deplores on Ennius' behalf the fact that Ennius' programmatically announced revolution in poetic technique

---

[34] On Daedalic numinousness see Gordon (1979), 8; cf. Morris (1992), 248, with Pausanias 2.4.5 Δαίδαλος δὲ ὁπόσα εἰργάσατο, ἀτοπώτερα μέν ἐστιν ἐς τὴν ὄψιν, ἐπιτρέπει δὲ ὅμως τι καὶ ἔνθεον τούτοις 'all the statues made by Daedalus, while somewhat odd to the view, are nevertheless distinguished by a kind of divine inspiration.'

[35] White (1987). Details remain controversial, especial points of contention being Horace's position *vis à vis* the *critici* and the interpretation of the tricky *leviter*. Cf. M. Barchiesi (1962), 40–50 and 62–70, Brink (1963–82) and Rudd (1989) ad loc. with bibl.; Rudd obelizes *leviter*.

means so little to Augustan readers that they are no less disposed to admire Naevius, whose poetry Ennius had claimed to supersede, than Ennius himself (*Epist.* 2.1.50–4):

> Ennius, et sapiens et fortis et alter Homerus,
> ut critici dicunt, leviter curare videtur
> quo promissa cadant et somnia Pythagorea.
> Naevius in manibus non est et mentibus haeret
> paene recens? adeo sanctum est vetus omne poema

> Ennius, though sage and bold – a second Homer, as the professors say – seems frivolous for worrying about the upshot of his pronouncements and Pythagorean dreams:[36] is not Naevius open in our hands and echoing in our heads as if he had written yesterday? So revered is every hoary poem. (tr. White)

The last line, with its *adeo sanctum est vetus omne poema*, sends us forward again to Quintilian and his *sacros vetustate lucos* for *post eventum* corroboration: it is indeed Ennius' fate to become part of the same undifferentiated antique world as his predecessor.

It may be suggested (rather against the grain of Horace's view of things, but with an eye to Cicero's rebuke of Ennius a third of a century earlier) that there is some (poetic) justice in this: a poet who perhaps overestimated the extent to which he had transformed and freed himself from the terms of reference of his predecessors suffers the ignominy of having his revolution underestimated, or wholly ignored, by later generations for whom the features which he has in common with his predecessors are more noticeable and significant than the features which differentiate him from them. As modern historians of Roman literature, we can learn both from Ennius' own tendentious claims of newness and from (equally) tendentious Augustan assimilations of Ennian poetry to undifferentiated oldness. We can use each kind of reading as a control on the other; and (as in my 'strong' proposition at the end of section 1) we can even play them off against each other so as to call into question the progressivist assumptions which they share.

Note, incidentally, that for Horace, an even firmer follower of the progressivist model than Cicero (and no less formative than he of

---

[36] *somnia Pythagorea*: i.e. Ennius' literary manifesto in *Ann.* 1. *promissa* may be felt to include the declarations in the *Ann.* 7 proem too: White (1987), 228n.3.

twentieth century narratives of Roman literary history), Augustan reverence for the poetic technique of Livius Andronicus represents the *reductio ad absurdum* of the undifferentiated craze for the archaic (*Epist.* 2.1.71–5). Not that even Horace is ruthless enough to seek to expunge Livius altogether from the literary historical record (69–71):

> *non equidem insector* delendaque carmina Livi
> esse reor, memini quae plagosum mihi parvo
> Orbilium dictare . . .

I am not in hostile pursuit of Livius' poems as fit only for deletion – poems which I remember Orbilius beating into me as a boy . . .

What most modern readers take from this anecdote is a condescending sense (Horace's, then complicitously their own) of Livius' verse as a mere prep school oddity. Condescension there is, but perhaps not quite as facile as it appears at first glance. One might better bring away from the passage Horace's punning allusion (which seems to have been missed) to the *incipit* line of the *Odusia*:

> virum mihi, Camena,   *insece* versutum

Horace perverts Livius' *incipit*; but, more than that, his means of doing so (an impish gloss of a much-discussed Livian rarity)[37] suggests that he expects his readers, like himself, to earn their right to condescend to a poet who (as he grudgingly admits in 73–4) still has a couple of words and lines worthy of the attention of a *doctus lector*.

In my third commentary, Gellius 12.2, the possibility of reading Ennius as a new poet to someone else's old poet seems wholly to have receded. He is an archaic poet: the issue is whether we admire or despise archaic poets. The chapter is a discussion of opinions expressed by the

[37] Horace's *insector* 'I pursue (with hostile words)' plays on an interpretation of *insece* which associates it with (non-hostile) narrative 'tracking': cf. a *grammaticus* reported in Gell. 18.9.3 who, arguing for the spelling *inseque*, glosses the word with *perge dicere* 'go on to tell' and *insequere* 'track, follow up'. The Gellian passage testifies to lively ancient debate concerning both orthography and meaning of *insece*; cf. also Paul. Fest. 99. Modern philologists derive *insece*, *inquam* and Homer's ἔννεπε from a root *sek^w– 'say' homonymous with but distinct from the root *sek^w– 'follow'. Horace's gloss aptly complements his reference to Orbilius, a noted grammarian and an expert in Ennian scholarship (Brink (1963–82) ad loc. with Suet. *Gram.* 8–9).

Younger Seneca (i.e. a century prior to Gellius) concerning Ennius and his reception in literary history, and thus dramatizes within itself fluctuations of taste between a number of different readers and reading communities: the Antonine writer, true to his age, is reverent towards Ennius;[38] his Neronian predecessor, at least in the Antonine's (tendentious) excerpting, is not. In Gellius' first example (12.2.3–5), Seneca criticizes Cicero for his praise of certain 'ridiculous verses', *deridiculos versus*, which Ennius had devoted to M. Cornelius Cethegus (=*Ann.* 306–8 Sk.). Seneca includes a delightful speculation concerning Cicero's motives in praising such Ennian lines (ap. Gell. 12.2.5):

' . . . nisi forte Cicero summus orator agebat causam suam et volebat suos versus videri bonos'

' . . . unless perhaps Cicero, that consummate orator, was pleading his own cause and wished his own verse to look good'.

Despite Gellius' outrage – below he terms Seneca a 'trifler', *homo nugator* – this caricature does put its finger on an undoubted truth, viz the self-interested spirit which (as we have seen) can underlie a Ciceronian narrative of literary history.

Next in Gellius' report, Cicero (sections 6–9) and Virgil are both castigated by Seneca for allowing Ennianisms into their own styles: this time Seneca blames not the author but the audience for dragging the author down to its own level. Thus on Virgil (10):

'Vergilius quoque noster non ex alia causa duros quosdam versus et enormes et aliquid supra mensuram trahentes interposuit, quam ut Ennianus populus agnosceret in novo carmine aliquid antiquitatis'

'Our Virgil too admitted certain verses which are harsh, irregular and somewhat beyond the proper measure, with no other motive than that a community devoted to Ennius might recognize some flavour of antiquity in the new poem.'

Note the multiple layers of taste represented here. An Antonine who reveres Ennius as archaic reports a Neronian who despises Ennius as

---

[38] Gellius does not fetishize the archaic as unconditionally as do some of his contemporaries. However, 'reverent' is a fair description here – as also of Gellius' praise for *Ann.* 268–86 Sk. at 12.4.

archaic reporting the strategy of an Augustan who knows better but is under pressure from other Augustans who revere Ennius as archaic. As modern readers, distant from all the interests and partialities of these and other groups of readers competing across generations and within the same generation (but perhaps with academic interests and partialities of our own), with which vantage-point in the history of Ennius-reception should we align ourselves, and why?

But it is on Seneca's pithiest dig at Ennius' old-fashioned status that I wish to dwell – more lingeringly than does the affronted Gellius (12.2.11):

> sed iam verborum Senecae piget; haec tamen inepti et insubidi hominis ioca non praeteribo: 'quidam sunt' inquit 'tam magni sensus Q. Ennii, ut, *licet scripti sint inter hircosos*, possint tamen inter unguentatos placere'

> But I am now weary of quoting Seneca; yet I shall not pass by the following jokes of that tasteless and foolish man: 'There are certain thoughts in Quintus Ennius', says he, 'that are of such great worth that though written among the unwashed, they nevertheless can find favour among the anointed.'

For Propertius and Ovid, Ennius is *hirsutus* as a poet; for Seneca he writes *inter hircosos*: a deliberate punning intensification of the Augustan insult may be suspected.[39] In Ovid's handling of the *Annales* at *Trist.* 2.259–60, *nihil est hirsutius illis* goes beyond stylistic denigration to mock the rustic air of the Ennian world at large; with Seneca's *hircosus* that air ripens into pungency.

As already noted in connexion with the *Tristia* passage, the effect of such judgements by urbane posterity is inevitably to collapse Ennius back into the world of his predecessors. A little more interpretative pressure can be applied to Seneca's jest in this connexion. To place Ennius and his writings *inter hircosos* is to place them, literally, among those of a 'goatish' aroma, among goatish men. But this is the very group which Ennius himself had characterized in his own poetic programme – and claimed to supersede (*Ann.* 206–7 Sk.):

---

[39] Assonantal and conceptual affinity between *hirsutus* and *hircosus*: cf. Hor. *Epod.* 12.5 *an gravis hirsutis cubet hircus in alis* 'or a rank he-goat lodges in the hirsute armpits'.

scripsere alii rem
vorsibus quos olim *Fauni* vatesque canebant

Fauni: creatures like Faunus, deity of the Italian woods, in form half-man . . . and half he-goat.[40] Seneca's witticism is not just another generalized case of posterity riding roughshod over the modernizing aspirations of Ennius' poetry, but a very specific perversion of the letter of his poetic in the *Annales* 7 proem (perhaps missed as such by Gellius, to whom Seneca is here merely inept).

On his own narrative Ennius triumphantly supersedes the *Fauni*; on Seneca's he can free himself only intermittently from their goatish world. It is clear that the *unguentati* are to be found in Seneca's time, not in Ennius', and that only on occasion, by special pleading, will Ennian poetry be able to shake off the aroma of archaic Rome.

To modify my initial description of the Gellian commentary, then, it turns out that 12.2 shows Seneca (at least) not wholly oblivious to Ennius' claim to be a new poet *vis à vis* Naevius. However, this does not prompt any reinstatement of Ennius' version of literary history. Rather, Seneca's reading denies the Ennian claim, or relativizes it to a point where it becomes a trivial distinction within a debate in which larger and (to a Neronian) more immediate distinctions are at stake.

Let us leave Gellius on Seneca on Ennius on Naevius with a healthy sense of the provisionality of any narrative of literary historical change, and turn our inquiry towards one particular group of Roman poets which, through an especially strong narrative in later twentieth century scholarship, has in our time attained a status almost beyond provisional-ity, beyond the vicissitudes of literary history, forever eclipsing its poetic predecessors and forever resisting assimilation to them: the (still) so-called 'New Poets' of the mid first century BCE.

3   New poets

If these *poetae novi* have become forever new, so their predecessors seem now fated to be forever predecessors. This section will sketch out an

---

[40] Ov. *Fast.* 5.101 *semicaper . . . Faune*; cf. Apuleius' description of Faunus' cognate Pan as the *hircuosus deus* (*Met.* 5.25).

approach to the 'neoterics'[41] of the mid first century by reopening some of the fragmentary poetry in Latin which survives from the generations before Catullus, Cinna and the now-celebrated arrival of Parthenius of Nicaea – poetry which (unlike the fragments of the neoterics themselves) seems to have been relegated to the closed stacks of literary history. These so-called predecessors are not wholly forgotten in the modern academy – the cult of the fragment is enough by itself to keep them visible – but they are characteristically invoked by critics interested in placing them in a narrative in which the 'New Poets' render them obsolete. It should be possible to envisage a little space for, e.g., Lutatius Catulus outside a narrative of pure obsolescence – Catulus, whose fate in literary history (not least in the chapter of Gellius, 19.9, which preserves his version of a Callimachean epigram) is to be 'not-Catullus'. However, the present discussion will concentrate on some rehabilitation for Laevius, a poet whose thirty-odd fragments give him a firmer evidential claim than Catulus to consideration, and who has been consistently downplayed in the past thirty years so as to throw his successors into higher relief.[42] Cicero will also be part of the story, as he is part of most stories about the late republic.

Thus far my chapter has taken its bearings mainly from ancient poets and critics; here I shall begin in the first instance from the academic criticism of the 1960s and since. At least until the final paragraphs of the section, my terms will be no less neotericentric than those I seek to revise: my interest here is in questioning the extremity of the cult of the new as manifested in this literary historical aetiology, not in abandoning the aetiological approach itself.

---

[41] *poetae novi*, νεώτεροι: since my section is as much about modern perceptions of the neoterics as about the neoterics' own self-perceptions, I register, but conditionally, the usual cautions about (mis)using Cicero's loaded terms (*Orat.* 161, *Att.* 7.2.1 respectively) to identify and label such a group: see most recently Courtney (1993), 189, with bibl., for the interpretation of νεώτεροι as 'epigones'; cf. also the more nuanced discussion of Lyne (1978), 167–9, ending ' . . . whatever Cicero thought, the poets themselves may well have considered that they were prophets of a "new poetry"'. Cicero's ability to dictate our literary historical terms again commands respect – however appropriative our readings of his readings of 'new poetry' may be.

[42] The *testimonia* of Laevius do not extend to precise evidence for dating, esp. if Kaster (1992), 41–5, is right to discount fr. 31 Courtney. The best approximation will still place his *floruit* c. 90 BCE: Courtney (1993), 118.

Recent literary historians, even when they do not actually use the word 'revolution' (which they often do), tend to characterize the poetry of the neoterics in terms of discontinuity with previous writing in Latin rather than of continuity.[43] Predecessors at Rome, including most importantly Laevius, are invoked in critical discussions not to make points about their closeness to the neoterics, but to make points about their distance from the neoterics. (Laevius' stock actually went down during the neoteric boom of the 1960s and 1970s.) Filling the void in many accounts is the Hellenic figure of Parthenius, through whom the neoterics find their true continuity: namely, continuity with Alexandria and more precisely with Callimachus, whom Parthenius brings front and centre for the first time in a direct line of Hellenic influence treated as independent of what has been going on at Rome before Parthenius' arrival.

I do not wish to argue here against this way of reading first century literary history, only to relativize it. I think it likely, in fact, that the neoterics themselves would have substantially agreed with this version. Wendell Clausen, in his influential argument for strong neoteric discontinuity with previous writing in Latin, is extrapolating from signals of a like attitude in Catullus himself. Nor do I wish to call into question the evidence for high valuation of Parthenius by the neoterics, which can indeed reasonably (in many respects if not in all) be inferred from the available hints.[44] My purpose is simply to offer a reminder that there is more to the question than the partial and interested views of the neoterics themselves. It seems to me that the problem with most modern characterizations of the neoteric 'moment' (going back to the compelling reconstruction in Clausen's 1964 essay) is not that they are untrue to how the neoterics thought of themselves, but that they are probably all too true. What we now have to do is to put some space between what the neoterics are known or (more often) are conjectured to have thought of their literary predecessors at Rome, and how we, benefiting (as well as losing) from the greater distance of our two millennia from them, assess the cultural currents of Hellenism in circulation in Rome at the time.

So, for example, when we find the tortured erotic themes of neoteric

---

[43] An early and notable exception is Crowther (1971).

[44] Clausen (1964) is the landmark discussion of Parthenius and Roman poetry; elaborations and qualifications in Wiseman (1974); Crowther (1976); Lyne (1978), esp. 186–7.

epyllion and other mythological narrative explained in terms of the
influence of Parthenius, even if we accept this as importantly true (there
is good reason to), we should relativize it – we should fill out parts of the
picture which the neoterics themselves might or might not think it
important to fill out.

Thus T.P. Wiseman lists among fragmentary neoteric epyllia reflective
of Parthenian concerns the *Glaucus* of Cornificius (fr. 2–3 Courtney),
adducing both Callimachus' Γλαῦκος, a title recorded by the *Suda*, and
the teasingly apt survival of a Greek hexameter by Parthenius himself
which catalogues the names Glaucus, Nereus and Melicertes (quoted by
Gellius 13.27.1–2 as the source of Virgil, *Geo.* 1.437). But in this literary
historical contextualization of the *Glaucus* Wiseman does not adduce the
fact that, some twenty years before Parthenius' arrival, Cornificius'
fellow-orator Cicero had already, in his early youth, come up with a
Roman *Pontius Glaucus* in trochaic verse (Plut. *Cic.* 2.3) – very likely in
imitation of Callimachus' poem, and without any need of mentorship
from Parthenius.[45]

So too the *Zmyrna* of Parthenius' importer Cinna[46] is commonly – and
surely rightly – inferred to be indebted to the Nicaean poet, whom we
know to have handled the Adonis myth (*SH* 641, 654). However, that
should not inhibit us as literary historians from registering the fact that,
presumably well before Parthenius' arrival in Rome, the Adonis myth
had also been handled by our unfashionable Laevius, in his metrically
and linguistically experimental collection of *Erotopaegnia*, or *Games of
Love* (fr. 6).

Now it may indeed be true that the neoterics themselves, like the
modern promoters of Parthenius, felt the author of the *Metamorphoses*
and *Erotica Pathemata* to be central to their inspiration, and the author
of the *Erotopaegnia* to be marginal. Clausen has made a strong case, with

---

[45] Wiseman (1974), 55 and n.68; his choice of a 'Parthenian' emphasis here is the more
marked in that Cicero's *Glaucus* is actually mentioned in another context earlier in
his essay (53). Cicero and Cornificius, whatever their disagreements on oratory
(*Fam.* 12.17.2) and politics, were by no means inhabitants of different worlds, at
least in the 40s: *Fam.* 12.17–30 collects Cicero's side of their correspondence
between 46 and 43 BCE.

[46] Accepting (with Wiseman (1974), 47–50) that it is 'Cinna the poet' whom the *Suda*
(quoted later) describes as acquiring Parthenius among the booty of Mithridates'
defeat (i.e. probably in 66 BCE rather than upon the capture of Nicaea in 73); it must
at least have been a kinsman.

the help of the 'Satrachan' connexion, for regarding Parthenius as Cinna's mentor in the composition of the *Zmyrna*;[47] perhaps Cinna was no more interested than are recent historians of neotericism[48] in the fact that Laevius had written on the same myth too.

On the other hand, the only 'New Poet' to survive in more than fragments, Catullus, does seem to me to offer a clear acknowledgement of the priority of Laevius when he embarks on the celebrated *exemplum* of Laodamia and Protesilaus in his ambitious elegy 68 – an extended passage aptly characterized by R.O.A.M. Lyne as 'a Catullan version of the sort of whimsically told mythological narrative which Callimachus fitted into the *Aetia*'.[49] David Ross writes (of Laevius in general) that while 'Catullus and the New Poets must have read Laevius with some interest', the 'notion of a debt to [him] would never have entered Catullus' mind'.[50] Perhaps that is right; but it is very tempting to read the splendid juxtaposition of names in the three-word pentameter which announces Catullus' Laodamia *exemplum* (68.73–4)

> coniugis ut quondam flagrans advenit amore
> *Protesilaeam Laodamia* domum

> As once upon a time ablaze with love for her husband came Laodamia to the house of Protesilaus

as an allusive acknowledgement of the distinctive title of Laevius' poem on this myth in the *Erotopaegnia* collection (fr. 13–19): *Protesilaodamia*.[51] One might even read the hexameter's *quondam* (like a *fama est*) as 'annotating' this specific evocation of poetic tradition.

A rereading of Ross's brilliant discussions in *Style and Tradition in Catullus* (1969) will find him arguing against continuities of style and

---

[47] *SH* 641 (*Etym. Gen.* s.v. Ἄδωος) locates Parthenius' interest in the Adonis myth at the river 'Setrachus', named only four times in ancient literature; Catullus' epigram on the *Zmyrna*, evidently offering the conceit that Cinna's epyllion will be read even as far away as the remote river which it celebrates, predicts (95.5) *Zmyrna cavas Satrachi penitus mittetur ad undas* '*Zmyrna* will be exported all the way to the caverned waves of Satrachus'. See Clausen (1964), 188–91.

[48] Again, a (cautious) exception is Crowther (1980), 181.

[49] Lyne (1978), 184.

[50] Ross (1969), 159, 160n.103.

[51] Hinds (1987b), 10n.7, was too tentative about this: cf. now Feeney (1992), 39n.36, who attractively conjectures further areas of Laevian influence on Catull. 68. On the distinctive haplology of the Laevian title see Courtney (1993) on fr. 19.

approach which were assumed by earlier twentieth century critics to exist between Laevius and Catullus. There is an element of virtuosic tendentiousness in Ross's treatment which seems to have been missed by more recent critics who have flattened it into textbook orthodoxy.[52] One must admire anew the tendentiousness (which – again – reads uncannily like the tendentiousness of Catullus' own polemical style in other contexts), but it is perhaps time for a compensatory reminder of some of the concurrences of interest between Laevius on the one hand and Catullus and the neoterics on the other, which struck earlier modern critics: polymetric variety (even given important differences in the metres and range of experiment involved[53]); use of diminutives and compounds (even granted that Laevian linguistic exuberance is in the final analysis *sui generis*); a Hellenistic tender-sentimental manner; and exploration of erotic themes in myth. Such concurrences are real enough to merit more discussion than they have received in recent decades. Laevius attracted the attention of later ancient scholars with words as bizarre as (ap. Gell. 19.7 = fr. 7–9) *trisaeclisenex* and even *subductisupercilicarptores*;[54] but against this novelty-store Laevius should be set the Laevius fragmentarily glimpsed in Andromache's chaplet for Hector (fr. 4),

> te Andromacha per ludum manu
> lascivola ac tenellula[55]
> capiti meo, trepidans libens,
> insolita plexit munera

Andromache in sport, hesitant, happy, with playful and tender little hand plaited you for my head, an uncommon gift

in the desire which (somehow) intensifies the sad death of Protesilaus (fr.

---

[52] See esp. Ross (1969), 156 'While it cannot be denied that [Laevius'] experiments with meter may have interested Catullus or that his vocabulary does resemble that characteristic of Catullus' polymetric poems, it must be argued here that too much emphasis has been placed on circumstantial similarities. A list of the parallels in the vocabulary of two poets, however long and however close the similarities, will not suffice to prove a dependent relation if their intentions and sources can be demonstrated to be entirely different.' The point about 'intentions' is especially pertinent to my discussion below.

[53] Laevian profusion *versus* neoteric concentration in metrical innovation: see (with some differences of emphasis) Ross (1969), 156–8, and Courtney (1993), 118–20.

[54] 'Triple-aged-elder'; 'eyebrow-raising-fault-finders'.

[55] The double diminutive *tenellulus*, first attested here, reappears only at Catull. 17.15.

19), *cupidius miserulo obito*, or in the favour informally asked of an everyday girlfriend (fr. 28), *mea Vatiena, amabo* – this last a locution familiar from comedy, but readily paralleled too in Catullus' (32.1) *amabo, mea dulcis Ipsitilla* 'please, my sweet Ipsitilla'.

However much or little the neoterics valued the poetry of Laevius, it was indubitably 'there' in the background; and as literary historians we should see that as part of the cultural matrix of neotericism – even if the neoterics themselves did not or (more plausibly) did not always do so. If there was a Parthenian revolution, or some other new and radical accession of Hellenistic influence in the wake of the Mithridatic Wars,[56] it happened within a reading community which was already in many important ways in a position to measure and to contextualize any new epiphany of Hellenism which a Parthenius could offer. The poetry of Laevius will have helped to determine, to construct, how a Parthenius was viewed and read upon arrival.

And if it really is the case that the neoterics themselves regarded Laevius as marginal, where Parthenius was central, then *even* as students of the neoterics' own views our job involves more than simply buying into that occlusion: to study the blind spots in a poet's image of the influences working upon him may be as revealing as to study the debts which he acknowledges.[57]

For another, even briefer attempt to relativize the neoteric moment, I want to consider the epiphany of Parthenius in terms of the traditional role of the Greek 'mentor' in Roman narratives of literary Hellenization. The interaction of the Greek (usually a man of letters, a philosopher or poet) with the Roman (usually a man, or men, of action) is a recurrent pattern in stories which Rome tells about itself;[58] the prestige of the cultural capital which the Greek brings to the table is balanced by the Roman's characteristic advantage in power. It is no great stretch to

---

[56] On this broader formulation Labate (1990), 927–31, is excellent.

[57] Familiar territory, of course, to the post-Bloomian critic: cf. the eye-opening suggestion in Krevans (1993), 156, that Callimachus had a blind spot for the influence of Antimachus' *Lyde* on his own *Aetia*; also Tanner (1993), quoting Isobel Armstrong on 'the heavy silence surrounding [Victorian poetry] in the twentieth century as a striking cultural phenomenon in itself'. The Bloomian possibilities in Ennius' *Ann.* 7 proem are outlined in Aicher (1989) – anticipated, of course (section 2 above), by Cicero.

[58] – and in stories which Greece tells about Rome. Cf. Pelling (1989) and Rawson (1989).

extend this pattern to the interaction of Parthenius and the 'New Poets': the figure most closely associated with Parthenius, Cinna, exemplifies another pattern (not unrelated to the first) according to which the Roman lives the life of letters within a life of action; and on the most probable inference (n.46 above) Cinna's encounter with Parthenius arose directly from his public career: (*SH* 605 [*Suda*]) οὗτος ἐλήφθη ὑπὸ Κίννα λάφυρον, ὅτε Μιθριδάτην Ῥωμαῖοι κατεπολέμησαν· εἶτα ἠφείθη διὰ τὴν παίδευσιν 'Parthenius was taken as a prize by Cinna when the Romans defeated Mithridates; then he was freed because of his learning'.

The pattern of interaction thus delineated constitutes a *topos* in Roman culture – but a *topos* which people could and did live by. The mixture of reality and self-fashioning in stories of Hellenic mentorship can make it hard to analyse the historicity and importance of such Greek/Roman pairings. Let me briefly diagram a few examples (Hellenic figure on the left in each case):

Andronicus / family of Livii[59]
Crates and Carneades / lecture audiences in mid 2nd century Rome[60]
Panaetius / Scipio Aemilianus
Archias / Lucullus and Catulus
Antiochus / Lucullus
Parthenius / Cinna and neoterics (plus Gallus and Virgil in next generation[61])

One further pairing, famously impugned by Cicero, may help to focus the problem of historicity:

Pythagoras / Numa[62]

Mention of Cicero cues a quick parenthesis. In the context of the present chapter's concern with the partiality of all versions of literary

---

[59] On Livius Andronicus as educator of Livian children see Jer. *Chron. Olymp.* 148.2; as teacher at Rome on a broader scale, Suet. *Gramm.* 1; cf. Gruen (1990), 82–3.

[60] See Suet. *Gramm.* 2 with Feeney (1991), 101, on Crates' embassy from Pergamum (168 BCE?) and broken leg; Gruen (1990), 174–7, on the 'philosophic embassy' from Athens (155 BCE).

[61] See Parth. *Erot. Path. praef.* (Gallus) and Macrob. *Sat.* 5.17.18 (Virgil).

[62] A meeting acknowledged as traditional but denied as a chronological impossibility at Cic. *De Orat.* 2.154 and *Rep.* 2.28–9; still a potent myth for Ovid at *Met.* 15.1–481. Cf. Gruen (1990), 158–70, a rich treatment.

history, it is worth stressing how many of the above pairings feature in our modern accounts because of the dominant influence of this one man's writings on the ways in which Roman republican literary history is even now framed. Cicero it is who most memorably extols Greek literary mentorship at Rome; and it is clear that his narratives are implicitly teleological and appropriative, tending towards a characterization and defence of his own philhellenism. To some extent, then, our modern readings of the mentorship pattern will find it difficult to avoid being contaminated by an element of storytelling towards a Ciceronian present.[63]

To resume: this sample catalogue of Greek/Roman pairs brings me back to the deliberately overstated terms of my 'strong' proposition (section 1). Should the several dialogues represented here be regarded unreservedly as a progressive series of steps in the Hellenizing of Roman culture – progressing towards some Augustan (or Ciceronian) *telos* – or is there a sense in which they should be read as a recurrent but essentially static pattern of mythic reenactment and reaffirmation, wherein every group of cultured Romans 'needs' a Greek mentor to validate its dialogue with Greece?

How far should we relativize the impact of Parthenius upon a Rome which had already played host to an Archias for more than a generation, the Rome of Laevius, the Rome in which the young Cicero could write a post-Callimachean *Glaucus* and a Latin *Aratea*, the latter several years before Cinna (fr. 11 Courtney) made the importation of an exquisite copy of Aratus from Bithynia into a neoteric position-statement?[64] Was the cultural importance of Parthenius something which the neoterics, whether all or some, just had to believe in to define themselves as

---

[63] This is to historicize, after Kennedy (1993), 10, the textualist definition of history as 'a kind of storytelling towards the present, that is, a textual construct at once itself an interpretation and itself open to interpretation'; cf. Felperin (1990), 142–69 at 159. For Ciceronian discussion of mentors named above see *De Orat.* 2.154–5 (Pythagoras, Carneades, and 'most learned Greeks' in the entourage of Scipio); *Mur.* 66, *Rep.* 1.15, *Att.* 9.12.2 (Panaetius); *Acad.* 2.4–6 (Panaetius and Antiochus); *Arch.*, esp. 5–6 (Archias). On the tendentiousness of intellectual portraits in Cicero's dialogues cf. Zetzel (1972), esp. 175–6, citing *Att.* 13.16.1, in which Cicero reveals his hand in the case of the *Academica*. More than two centuries later Cicero himself, in exile, is furnished with a Greek adviser by Cassius Dio (38.18–29), in a narrative with fascinating teleologies of its own: Gowing (1997).

[64] On Cinna fr. 11 cf. G.D. Williams (1992), 179–80.

innovators in Roman culture? To put the question at its strongest, and
à la Pierre Bourdieu,[65] if Parthenius had not existed, would the neoterics
have had to invent him – to be their Pythagoras, and to validate the
newness and prestige of their Hellenizing revolution?

4   Change and 'decline'

I have focussed thus far on narratives of innovation and progress. Roman
poetry also offers its literary historical tales of decline and decadence, of
which the most famous and enduring is the one told about poets of the
so-called 'Silver Age' of Latin literature (remember, however, as an
immediate caution against too easy a periodization, that on Cicero's
reading the 'New Poets' themselves were not so much 'new' as 'epigonal':
n.41 above). The 'Silver' label, which is post-antique,[66] plots the literature
of the early centuries CE as a falling away from the perfection of the high
Augustan era, constructed thus as a 'Golden Age' – in evident complicity
with the visionary rhetoric of Augustan myth-making itself.[67]

As in the previous section, I begin from the literary scholarship of our
own time. In Dublin in the later 1970s, the undergraduate classicist
undertook a four-year syllabus of reading courses which invited the
inference that a grounding in Roman poetry might reasonably end with
the death of Horace: Juvenal (the usual exception) was the sole post-
Augustan poet prescribed, and verse datable after the start of the Com-
mon Era was otherwise represented by a single book of Ovid's *Meta-
morphoses* anomalously appended to a course on Horace's *Odes*. Such
practical recognition of a debasement of Latin poetry in or around the last
decade BCE was fairly standard in Anglophone classics departments; and
the literary critical bibliography of the time reflects a similar emphasis.

Concerted attempts to recuperate post-Horatian and post-Virgilian
poetry have now been under way for a generation. Ovid, even the Ovid

---

[65] For Bourdieu's (1984) 'cultural capital' in the context of Roman Hellenization cf.
Edwards (1993), 22–4.

[66] To grammarians of the Roman empire from Probus to Servius, authors more recent
than Virgil were (again) *neoterici*, with the same shading available as has been
inferred for Cicero's νεώτεροι; on the question of their treatment in Servius see
Kaster (1978). The earliest *OED* entry for 'Silver Age' Latin finds the term already
standard in 1736.

[67] Cf. Virg. *Ecl.* 4.4–9, *Aen.* 6.791–4; Zanker (1988), 167–92 and refs.

of the *Fasti* and exile poetry, has been fully readmitted to the Augustan canon, Lucan is being treated as a major poet, and most recently Statius is leading the Flavians in from the cold. There is no lack of energy in all this recuperation; but there is some lack of consensus as to its terms and strategies.

A widespread (and often enabling) approach has been to treat the fixation on decline (and on the related issue of 'secondariness', to be discussed in section 5) as an aberration of academic criticism, and to read, say, Lucan and Statius (for I shall concentrate on these) as self-evidently first-rate writers who have been wilfully misunderstood through a narrow classicizing prejudice in modern scholarship. Testimonials from major poets in the Western tradition are often invoked to reproach the modern academy for its myopia in this matter: it is pointed out that Lucan and Statius enjoyed from the likes of Dante and Chaucer the respect and attention which is denied them by professors of Roman literature.

But no sooner does this reformist approach get under way than a vigorous counter-reformation is launched in Gordon Williams's *Change and Decline* (1978). This book (based on the Sather lectures of 1973) begins by issuing a strong reminder that the idea of decline is not simply a piece of modern superstructure to be thrown away at will: writers in the 'Silver Age' persistently characterize *themselves* as living in a period of cultural decadence. Williams's opening chapter is entitled 'Contemporary analyses of decline'; his book as a whole promotes the position that we would do better to heed – and, importantly, to extend – such analyses, than to embrace the literature of the period with 'the present-day attitude of permissiveness, that finds virtue in any writer (given a sufficient "understanding" of him)'.[68]

Now, if the 'permissive' approach has continued to gather momentum since 1978, while *Change and Decline* has been treated as something of a blind alley, that is in part because the book seems so polemically determined to eschew generosity in its readings of the writers studied, most dramatically Ovid. Critics who expect their poets to succeed tend to tell better stories than critics who expect their poets to fail; and to many

---

[68] I quote from the dust-jacket, to show how readily this counter-reformation can be fitted ('paratextually': cf. Genette (1982), 9–10) with its own modern agenda. 'Permissiveness' is a key term in G. Williams's (1978) introduction; '[confront] the present-day attitude of . . . ', perhaps an editor's phrase, heightens an emphasis in (1978), 1–2, in the direction of a broader language of societal alarmism.

readers the disenfranchisement of post-Horatian literature from the critical pluralism characteristic of Williams's own epoch-making *Tradition and Originality in Roman Poetry* (1968), though deliberate, has seemed in practice arbitrary, and Williams's appeals to standards and values consequently disingenuous.

However, in his initial historicization of the issue of literary decline Williams did indeed make an important point, which reformers ignore to their own detriment. The critic who disregards 'contemporary analyses of decline' in championing, say, Lucan may save the poet only at the cost of radically dehistoricizing him, so that what is restored is no more than a bloodless semblance of the Lucan who was lost.

There remains a further point of vulnerability in the programme of *Change and Decline*; and Lucan will serve as a test case. The fact is that, *where it counts*, Williams himself has done little more than the 'permissivists' to take that first step of locating Lucan (or any other poet) within Silver-Age discussions of decline and decadence. Despite its professions, the book's opening chapter has much of the feel of a reading from the outside: the 'contemporary analyses of decline' are gathered from overt theorizations of the period in moralizing prose, which are subsequently *applied* to the *practice* of 'Silver' writers, mainly poets, from Ovid onwards. What is missing here (and the omission has implications for Williams's project of extending his opening chapter's terms) is any sense of the poets' own self-conscious participation in these analyses, and hence of the *discursive* approach to decline which their work often demands. In Williams's account the Elder Seneca and the Elder Pliny theorize decline; Lucan simply declines. But Lucan himself can be argued to be one of the most powerful of all post-Augustan theorists of decline and decadence.[69] To miss this may be to miss the crux of the matter; and it is here that a new wave of recuperation has emerged, in the recent impressive flowering of Lucanian criticism. Decline for Lucan is now understood to be a *trope*, a trope central to his epic project: to put it in a postmodern nutshell, no analysis of Lucanian decline can get far without considering Lucanian "decline".[70]

To a chronicler of change and decline, *De Bello Civili* constitutes a

---

[69] So Johnson (1987), 123–34.

[70] Here and in section 5 I allow myself the licence of *double* quotation-marks to lend temporary emphasis to one particular deployment of this common typographical shorthand.

falling away from Virgilian perfection of epic technique; to a chronicler of change and "decline", *De Bello Civili* embraces the idea of a falling away from Virgilian perfection of epic technique as a powerful and enabling trope. A debased hero, Julius Caesar, whose sense of tradition is so deficient that, amid the rank weeds of a neglected Troy (9.969 'even the ruins are ruined' *etiam periere ruinae*), he has to be held back from unwittingly violating the sacred places of the city, trampling on the *manes* of Hector and blundering over the altar which saw, in *Aeneid* 2, the murder of Priam (9.975–9);[71] a theme which at its climax becomes too unspeakable to narrate (7.552–4),[72]

> hanc fuge, mens, partem belli tenebrisque relinque,
> nullaque tantorum discat me vate malorum,
> quam multum bellis liceat civilibus, aetas

> Flee, mind of mine, from this part of the war and leave it to darkness.
> I refuse to be the poet of such horrors: let no age learn from me the
> full licence of civil war

so that everything, including the normal decorum of epic battle narrative, breaks down in the face of it (7.617–20);[73]

> impendisse pudet lacrimas in funere mundi
> mortibus innumeris, ac singula fata sequentem
> quaerere, letiferum per cuius viscera volnus
> exierit, quis . . . [quis . . . quis . . . quis . . .]

> On the day the whole world died, it would be shameful to waste tears
> upon countless individual deaths, following fates one by one and
> asking, through whose vitals the death-dealing wound passed, who
> . . . (etc.)

a poet whose voice is so immoderate that his modern critics can variously accuse him of excessive obsequiousness to Nero, excessive hostility to Caesarism, and both in the same poem; an epic stripped of its traditional divine machinery and presided over by a new god of poetry, none other than Nero (1.63–6):

---

[71] On the import of the allusions to *Aen.* 2 in the description of Caesar's visit to Troy cf. Hardie (1993), 107. On the passage's debasement of Aeneas' visit to Pallanteum in *Aen.* 8 see Martindale (1993), 49–52.

[72] Feeney (1991), 276–7.   [73] Martindale (1993), 49.

sed mihi iam numen; nec, si te pectore vates
accipio, Cirrhaea velim secreta moventem
sollicitare deum Bacchumque avertere Nysa:
tu satis ad vires Romana in carmina dandas

But to me you [i.e. Nero] are a deity already; nor, if my breast receives
you to inspire my verse, would I wish to trouble the god who sways
Delphi's secrets, or to divert Bacchus from Nysa: you alone suffice to
give strength for Roman song

– such are some of the terms in which Lucan's epic can be mapped as an
epic of (self-conscious) "decline".

Let me dwell for a moment upon the persistently controversial matter
of the praise of Nero in Lucan's proem, represented in my last quotation.
'A seriously intended, but highly stereotyped tribute', as Williams would
have it, whose very inconsistency with the bitter attitude to Caesarism in
the rest of the poem bears witness to the aesthetic and moral failure
which causes poets of decline to think episodically and without regard
for the whole: 'this is another example of the way in which poets in this
period could take material and give it appropriate rhetorical treatment
without involving themselves in the truth or falsity of the subject mat-
ter'.[74] 'No', says the permissivist reading, taking the proem's invocation
of Nero as a patent *parody* of encomiastic rhetoric, and hence fully
consistent with Lucan's attitudes to Caesarism later in the poem. A
better response may be 'Yes, but . . . '.[75] The world of Lucanian epic *is* a
world in which failures of aesthetic and moral consistency are inevitable;
and that is precisely Lucan's point. The best commentary on the praise
of Nero may be the very denunciation of Caesarism later in the poem
which has seemed to many to be so irreconcilable with it (7.454–9):

> . . . mortalia nulli
> sunt curata deo. cladis tamen huius habemus
> vindictam, quantam terris dare numina fas est:
> bella pares superis facient civilia divos;
> fulminibus manes radiisque ornabit et astris
> inque deum templis iurabit Roma per umbras

[74] Williams (1978), 164.
[75] The following draws heavily on Feeney (1991), 297–301, and Johnson (1987),
118–23, and seeks to supplement Hinds (1987b), 26–9.

The human sphere has never been watched over by any god. Yet for this disaster we have revenge, as much as gods may give to mortals: the civil wars will put [Caesarian] *divi* on a par with the gods above. Decking out dead men with thunderbolts and rays and stars, Rome will swear by ghosts in the temples of the gods.

Mankind will get its revenge on the gods by allowing dead Caesars to usurp a share of their honours. This is a tale of debasement in the divine order; and it comes from a poet who has himself in the Book 1 proem celebrated in advance the post-mortem transformation of Nero into a god-supplanting heavenly body (1.47–8, 50–52),

> . . . seu sceptra tenere,
> seu te flammigeros Phoebi conscendere currus
> . . . iuvet, tibi numine ab omni
> cedetur, iurisque tui natura relinquet
> quis deus esse velis, ubi regnum ponere mundi

Whether it please you to hold Jupiter's sceptre, or to mount the flaming chariot of Phoebus . . . , every deity will yield to you, and Nature will leave it to you to decide which god you wish to be, and where to establish your universal throne

and who has invited that same Caesarian *divus* even in his lifetime (*sed mihi iam numen*) to usurp the vatic honours of Apollo and Bacchus. This is how things must be in the world after Pharsalus. Celebration of Nero and condemnation of Caesarism do indeed sit ill together in *De Bello Civili*, and that should be registered; but the breakdown in aesthetic and moral consistency is not without its self-conscious post-lapsarian logic. On the (re)reading of the proem opened up by 7.454–9, celebration of a Caesar is self-cancelling, and perverts itself into a bitter, imperfect joke through which alone the epicist of "decline" can damn the gods who allowed Caesarism to happen on their watch.[76]

---

[76] The appeal to Vacca's account of two-stage, pre- and post-ban composition, dismissed by Feeney (1991), 298n.192, but since reinstated by Fantham (1992), 13–14, and Dewar (1994), remains attractive to critics who seek to take the vocabulary of panegyric in the Book 1 proem at face value. However, as both these discussions allow, even on this view one may ask how the proem was reread by the now-disenchanted Lucan who wrote the later books of *De Bello Civili*. The very fact of *not* rewriting the Book 1 proem in the light of the evolving poem could itself facilitate a kind of 'rewriting', by provoking actively revisionist *recontextualization* of the passage in later books.

Like Lucan's *De Bello Civili*, the *Tristia* and *Epistulae ex Ponto* of Ovid have often been read as poetry which debases the currency of Golden Latin. This narrative of 'Silver' history, although in some respects peculiar to Ovid (erosion of previous creativity due to low morale in exile, lack of cultural and bibliographical resources at Tomis), in its tale of the victimization of a poet by an autocratic *princeps* has been felt to be more broadly symptomatic; so that the *Tristia* and *Epistulae ex Ponto* have been seen as foundational texts of the age of decline.

However, Ovid's elegies from exile, like Lucan's epic, are now being recuperated as poetry of "decline" (to deploy again my enhanced quotation-marks); and here too they perhaps deserve foundational status. The agenda is established very explicitly indeed in the opening column of *Tristia* I, as the poet addresses this first book written after the catastrophe of exile, sending it off to Rome as his surrogate (1.1.3–10):

> vade, sed incultus, qualem decet exulis esse;
>   infelix habitum temporis huius habe.
> nec te purpureo velent vaccinia fuco –
>   non est conveniens luctibus ille color –
> nec titulus minio, nec cedro charta notetur,
>   candida nec nigra cornua fronte geras.
> felices ornent haec instrumenta libellos;
>   fortunae memorem te decet esse meae

Go, but unadorned, as becomes the book of an exile; in your infelicity wear the style of dress appropriate to my present time. You should have no cover dyed with purple berry – no fit colour is that for mourning – neither should your title be tinged with vermilion nor your paper with oil of cedar; and no white horns on dark roll-ends. Let such accoutrements decorate books which enjoy felicity; my ill-fortune is what *you* should bear in mind.

What is being set up in these prescriptions to the book concerning its outward appearance is nothing less than a self-conscious decorum of decline; and in the poems which follow "decline" is indeed mobilized as one of Ovid's key tropes.

However, the Ovidian parallel, even as it illuminates the idea of "decline" as construct, can also help us to test the limits of that idea. The latest wave of discussion has been an exhilarating one, and especially congenial to a generation of critics (my own) whose readings owe something to the late twentieth century aesthetic which privileges meta-literary self-consciousness as its master-term. But it may be time to confront a new kind of literary historical absolutism. Whereas in the past Ovid's own professions of decline were taken as confirming an actual decline in his work, on the new postmodern reading the elaborate Ovidian manipulations of "decline" are increasingly being taken as a kind of proof that there is *no* decline in the exile poetry: the self-consciousness of the trope empties it of its meaning.

But Ovid's is a case which can expose the dangers of too facile a postmodern revisionism. Where the main lesson drawn in sections 1 and 3 above was 'Just because a poet says he has superseded his predecessors, that doesn't necessarily mean he has superseded his predecessors', in the present discussion we should emphasize, not only the parallel lesson, but also the complementary one which warns against too neat a revisionism in the first: i.e. not only 'Just because a poet says his work has declined, that doesn't necessarily mean his work has declined', but also 'Just because a poet says his work has declined, that doesn't necessarily mean it *hasn't* declined'. The new orthodoxy which privileges textual self-fashioning over biographical speculation risks missing the important – if unprovable – truth, discernible more between the lines of Ovid's exile poetry than in the never-faltering decorum of decline *in* the lines, that as the long years wear on Ovid *does* fall away from his peak as a poet. His exile books grow into their trope: "decline" becomes decline, and none of the newly appreciated virtuosity in Ovid's framing of his suffering should be allowed to devalue the suffering thus framed.

Nor, to return to our main example, would it be fair to Lucan to turn the dysfunctional world view of *De Bello Civili* into pure trope. That dysfunction is thematized in some of the most brilliant poetry in the Roman epic tradition; but to read it as sanitized by its quotation-marks, to deny to Lucan a pervasive sense of compromised artistic and moral integrity by reading it as a mere formalist gesture, might in the end produce no less unfair a reading of *De Bello Civili* than the reading which failed to see the dysfunction as a trope in the first place.[77] Recognition of the tropes of literary history does not entail denial of their status as lived experience. As for the poets, so for the modern historians of early

---

[77] This is to reconfirm Henderson's Lucanian (anti-)poetics at (1987), 123; cf. Martin-dale (1993), 68–9.

imperial literature, decline and "decline" are two terms which need each other; much of the characteristic energy of Lucanian epic, as of Ovidian exile elegy, depends upon the tension whereby these terms are neither wholly fused nor wholly separable.

5 'Secondary' epic

I group Ovid's elegies from Tomis and Lucan's *De Bello Civili* because in both cases an avowed decadence in their work is ascribed less to some inherent superiority of talent in their poetic predecessors than to a shift in the universe itself which has changed the rules under which poetry can operate. Ovid and Lucan come across, in fact, as two of the most artistically self-confident poets in Roman literature: Lucan's strongly appropriative intertextual imagination tends to implicate Virgil in Lucanian aetiologies of decline rather than leaving him on his pedestal[78] (and on the strict logic of Lucan's own narrative the *Aeneid*, as a product of the aftermath of the civil war, is itself a post-lapsarian epic); the exiled Ovid, not hesitating to figure his exile as a cosmic catastrophe, albeit on a smaller, elegiac scale (e.g. *Trist.* 1.8.1–10), is quite clear that Homer would have done no better than he if faced with a like situation (*Trist.* 1.1.47–8):

> da mihi Maeoniden et tot circumice casus,
> ingenium tantis excidet omne malis

> Give me Homer and cast just as many dangers about him; all his genius will fall away in the presence of such great ills.

For my chapter's other foray into the early empire, however, I turn to Statius, whose characterization of himself as a poet inferior in talent to his predecessors has seemed more unconditional, more matter-of-fact – and hence a greater embarrassment to those critics who now seek to recuperate him. Perhaps no verses have done more to keep all post-Augustan epic out of the modern academic canon than these, addressed by Statius to his *Thebaid* in that poem's closing column (12.816–17):

> vive, precor; nec tu divinam Aeneida tempta,
> sed longe sequere et vestigia semper adora

[78] See esp. Feeney (1986); Masters (1992), 128–33.

O live, I pray! and yet attempt not to rival the divine *Aeneid*, but
follow at a distance and ever worship its footsteps.

Small wonder that the scholarly orthodoxy should read thus (J.H.
Mozley, in his 1928 introduction to the Loeb Statius): 'To be the author
of a great epic poem is to count as one of the few great poets of the world,
and it need hardly be said that Statius can make no claim to that honour.
He stands with Apollonius, Lucan and Valerius Flaccus in the second
rank.' 'Can make no claim' and indeed, it seems, makes no claim. The
same self-depreciation characterizes an 'editorial' intervention in the
body of the epic too, Statius' post-Virgilian apostrophe to his latter-
day[79] Nisus and Euryalus, Dymas and Hopleus (10.445–8):

> vos quoque sacrati, quamvis mea carmina surgant
> inferiore lyra, memores superabitis annos.
> forsitan et comites non aspernabitur umbras
> Euryalus Phrygiique admittet gloria Nisi

> You too are exalted, though my songs rise from a more lowly lyre;
> you will survive the unforgetting years. Perhaps too Euryalus will not
> spurn you as comrade shades, and Phrygian Nisus in his glory will
> receive you.

Here, no less than in the *Thebaid* epilogue, the secondariness which the
condescension of old-style modern scholarship takes to be the normal
condition of Neronian and Flavian epic is something self-conscious –
self-conscious in its overtly deferential citation of its Virgilian model
(*Aen.* 9.446–9), self-conscious too, perhaps, in what may be a mannered
replication of the model-passage's line-position within its own book.[80]

Not just secondariness, then, but "secondariness", in terms of the
distinction discussed in section 4. The fact that the inferiority of the
Thebaid to the *Aeneid* is so carefully constructed by Statius should make
us ponder the value-judgement rather than merely internalizing it, as

---

[79] 'Latter-day' in the literary historical chronology of Roman epic but earlier, of
course, in mythic chronology: cf. chapter 4, section 3.
[80] So too Vessey (1986), 2966 n.3. Given the perils of transmission, the suggestion
cannot be ruled out of court because of a one-verse misalignment. 'Stichometric
intertextuality', an idea which becomes attractive if widespread use of line-numbers
in Roman poetic book-rolls is countenanced, is discussed in some ongoing work by
Don Fowler; he credits L. Morgan with the term. Cf. also Smith (1990).

Mozley has done ('it need hardly be said . . . ').[81] Note, first of all (and here at once is something to distinguish Statius' literary history from Mozley's), that in the *Genethliacon Lucani* (*Silvae* 2.7) Statius exempts Lucan's epic from the etiquette of deference to the *Aeneid* which he imposes on his own in the passages quoted above (79–80):

> quid? maius loquar: ipsa te Latinis
> Aeneis venerabitur canentem

> Why, I shall give greater praise. The *Aeneid* itself, as you sing to the Latins, shall pay you veneration.

The trajectory of the worship is presented in these lines as a reversal of expectation – and it is tempting to read the expectation being reversed as the very one expressed in *Theb.* 12.816–17, with its no less marked liturgical language (*divinam Aeneida*; *semper adora*).[82] An acknowledgement by Statius (ventriloquizing the Muse Calliope) of a poet who was less deferential than he in confronting the Virgilian paradigm?[83]

But more needs to be added to the picture. In another of the *Silvae*, thanking Vibius Maximus for his support, Statius exempts the *Thebaid* itself from the etiquette of deference to the *Aeneid*, and here his reversal of the *Thebaid*'s own epilogue ('*nec tu divinam Aeneida tempta*' 12.816) could hardly be clearer:

> quippe te fido monitore nostra
> Thebais multa cruciata lima
> *temptat* audaci fide Mantuanae
> gaudia famae   (*Silv.* 4.7.25–8)

---

[81] Contrast the canniness of Louis MacKay's epigram at the head of my chapter (source Pierre MacKay), which turns precisely on Statius' dramatization of his own secondariness.

[82] The completed *Thebaid* was already out when *Silv.* 1–3 was published as a collection (1 *praef.*; Coleman (1988), xvi–xvii); whether its epilogue had been framed when 2.7 was first composed must remain more uncertain.

[83] Cf. Hardie (1993), 110–11. Statius establishes (on his own account) a strong mood of *reverentia* towards Lucan in the preface to *Silvae* 2, explaining thus his choice of metre in poem 7 (the book's only non-hexametric poem): *ego non potui maiorem tanti auctoris habere reverentiam quam quod laudes eius dicturus hexametros meos timui* 'I could not show a deeper reverence for so great an author than by distrusting my own hexameters when about to sing his praises.'

For it is with you as loyal counsellor that my *Thebaid*, tortured by much use of the file, attempts with daring lyre the joys of Virgilian fame.

The effect is perhaps not so much to undercut the *Thebaid*'s prohibition as to reframe it, to emphasize its occasionality, an occasionality which complicates any attempt to read it as a literary historical position statement. Kathleen Coleman's note ad loc. is instructive: 'Whereas at *Theb.* 12.816–17 Statius was displaying conventional modesty in presenting his new work before the public, here the circumstances are different: if the credit is to be worth sharing with Vibius it must be exalted, and surely at the moment of resting from the genre Statius can take legitimate pride in its success.'

'Conventional' is always a troublesome word: it is the word on which the whole controversy concerning Lucan's praise of Nero turns. But one context in which the word 'conventional' does indeed suggest itself as an appropriate description of Statius' self-depreciation at the end of the *Thebaid* is the context offered by the very final scene in the poem's narrative, immediately before the epilogue; for what precedes that closing remark about the *Aeneid* is Statius' version of the classic image of epic (in)capacity, the 'many mouths' *topos*, applied to the funeral rites for the Argive dead (12.797–9):

> non ego, centena si quis mea pectora laxet
> voce deus, tot busta simul vulgique ducumque,
> tot pariter gemitus dignis conatibus aequem

> I could not, even if some god were to open out my breast with one hundred voices, match in worthy strains so many funerals of leaders alike and commoners, so many shared lamentations.

As we saw in chapter 2, poet after elevated poet, following the lead of Homer, had uttered that statement of incapacity; and in post-Homeric poetry it had commonly – at some level – had as a subtext 'If Homer couldn't do it, how can I?'. Here then is a reminder, through juxtaposition, not to be too definitive in labelling the self-depreciation of 12.816–17 as something new, and newly decadent, in Roman literature. One of the ways in which an epicist marks his genre as the highest and most ambitious is to stress his incomplete capacity to control it. In that context 816–17 can be read as offering an acknowledgement of the necessary limits of epic ambition analogous to the acknowledgement constituted by the preceding 'many mouths' *recusatio* at 797ff. To call this earlier passage a *topos* is not to foreclose interpretation either upon it (as chapter 2 should have demonstrated) or upon the passage which follows: if anything, the challenge to interpret each is sharpened by the juxtaposition.

A *topos*, then, which implicitly marks the secondariness of all epic to Homer is followed by an explicit statement of secondariness to Virgil. The juxtaposition encapsulates something distinctive to the dynamic of early imperial literature. As Roland Mayer has well argued, it was in the Neronian period (and in the Flavian period after it) that the Augustans became classics:[84] for the first time in Roman literature the texts invoked as foundational by a new writer were as likely to be Roman as Greek. As Homer had been to Virgil, so now was Virgil to his epic successors. Hence, partly, the title of my section, *"Secondary" epic*, chosen to suggest that that label, traditionally associated not with Statius but with Virgil, is always in practice (*pace* the oralists) open to relativization, reframing, appropriation to a new narrative of secondariness.[85]

It is noteworthy that, as the last column of Statius' *Thebaid* yields an overt expression of deference to Virgil, so the first column of his interrupted *Achilleid* yields an overt expression of deference to Homer (1.1–7):

> magnanimum Aeaciden formidatamque Tonanti
> progeniem et patrio vetitam succedere caelo,
> diva, refer. quamquam acta viri multum inclita cantu
> Maeonio (sed plura vacant), nos ire per omnem –
> sic amor est – heroa velis Scyroque latentem
> Dulichia proferre tuba nec in Hectore tracto
> sistere, sed tota iuvenem deducere Troia

> Tell, o goddess, of great-spirited Achilles, of the progeny feared by Jove and forbidden to inherit his father's heaven. Although the man's deeds are greatly celebrated in Homeric song (but more remains untold), grant me – for such is my desire – to take on the hero in his totality, to bring him forth from his hiding-place on Scyros with

---

[84] Mayer (1982), 317–18.

[85] For the textbook *ancient* designation of Virgil as '*secundus*' to Homer, cf. Domitius Afer ap. Quint. *Inst.* 10.1.86.

Ulysses' trumpet, and not to stop short at the dragging of Hector, but to lead the youth through the whole tale of Troy.

'[Statius] justifies his presumptuous choice of Homer's own hero by including those things that Homer does not narrate, i.e. the whole life of Achilles.'[86] Again the deferential gesture may not be entirely ingenuous. After the proem's assurances about how the rest of Achilles' life leaves Statius plenty of space in which to operate without competing with Homer, the poet's first move (1.20–94) is nothing less than a shot[87] right across Homer's bows: in a remake (or a 'prequel') of the act which sets the *Iliad*'s plot in motion in its first book, a complaining Thetis makes an appeal for a divine intervention in the Trojan narrative to help her son, addressed to a god who corresponds in this vignette to the *Iliad*'s Zeus (1.48–9):

> ibo tamen pelagique deos dextramque *secundi*,
> quod superest, complexa *Iovis* . . .

Yet I will go, and clasping the gods of the sea and (nought else remains) the right hand of second Jove . . .

Secundi . . . Iovis: is it possible that in this intertextual context the periphrasis for Neptune, itself conventional, self-consciously signals a moment of belatedness – with Neptune playing the role of *secundi . . . Iovis* to the 'original' Jove of the *Iliad*? This is, after all, the vocabulary to be expected from the poet whose previous epic defined itself as following a respectful 'second' behind another self-evidently inimitable model: *Theb.* 12.817 *sed longe sequere*; remember that *secundus* is an old participial form of *sequor*. That may be to press *Ach.* 1.48–9 too hard; or it may be to put a finger on a key term of Statian programmatics. What of the characterization of the *Achilleid* back in the proem as *fronde secunda* – with a pun[88] – to the *Thebaid*'s *primis . . . vittis*? (1.8–11)

---

[86] Hardie (1993), 63 (though, like others, he goes on to explore the Virgilian, rather than the Homeric dimensions of *Ach.* 1.20–94).

[87] Or a feint? Not enough of the *Achilleid* exists to tell us how persistent the challenge to Homer would have been. In the book and a quarter which we have, other agendas may be felt to dominate: see chapter 5 below.

[88] *Secunda* may initially translate either as 'second' (cf. line 8) or as 'propitious' (in the context of Apollo's support); the dominance of 'second' by the end of line 11 is guaranteed by the contrast with *primis . . . vittis*.

tu modo, si veterem digno deplevimus haustu,
da fontes mihi, Phoebe, novos ac fronde secunda
necte comas: neque enim Aonium nemus advena pulso
nec mea nunc primis augescunt tempora vittis

As for you, Phoebus, if with a worthy draught I drained the former fount, grant me new springs and bind my hair with a second chaplet: for not as a newcomer do I seek entrance to the Aonian grove, nor are these the first fillets to magnify my brow.

And does this connect to other kinds of secondariness and succession explored and problematized in the *Achilleid* proem, viz the denial to Achilles of the opportunity to succeed Jupiter in the dominion of the sky (1.1–2, quoted above), and (with a markedly different hierarchy of first and second) the status of the *Achilleid* as a mere preface to a future epic on Domitian?[89] (1.18–19)

. . . te longo necdum fidente paratu
molimur magnusque tibi praeludit Achilles

Yours is the theme which I labour to bring about with long but not yet confident preparation, and great Achilles plays prelude to you

– Domitian, who holds the ultimate option on primacy of all kinds, in poetic composition as well as in leadership? (1.14–16)

at tu, quem longe primum stupet Itala virtus
Graiaque, cui geminae florent vatumque ducumque
certatim laurus (olim dolet altera vinci)

But you, who are first by far in the admiring gaze of Italy's and Greece's finest, for whom the twin laurels of poet and general burgeon in mutual rivalry (one of them long since grieves to be outdone by the other) . . .

Is there a common thread of interest here at the beginning of the *Achilleid* in how authority is passed on from one epic character to the next, from one epic to the next, from one singer of epic to the next? It would take a bold reading to map out a fully coherent poetic here; but, if

---

[89] *Thebaid-Achilleid*-Domitianic epic as Statius' envisaged career-path: cf. also *Silv.* 4.4.87–100.

any of this speculation leads anywhere, Statian secondariness may be ready to enter dialogue with Statian "secondariness", and to move beyond embarrassment.[90]

[90] In the case of the *Thebaid* epilogue, a movement already well under way: add Henderson (1993), 163–4, 188; Malamud (1995), 21–7.

4

Repetition and change

unde quo veni? levis una mors est
virginum culpae

> (Horace, *Carmina* 3.27.37–8)

Whence, whither have I come? Too slight is one death for maidens' sin

levis una mors est – levis, at extendi potest

> ([Seneca,] *Hercules Oetaeus* 866)

Too slight is one death – too slight, but it can be drawn out

Wilde: 'I wish I had said that.'
Whistler: 'You will, Oscar, you will.'

> (from L.C. Ingleby, *Oscar Wilde*)

To be, in the twentieth century, a popular novelist of the seventeenth seemed to him a diminution. To be, in some way, Cervantes and reach the *Quixote* seemed less arduous to him – and, consequently, less interesting – than to go on being Pierre Menard and reach the *Quixote* through the experiences of Pierre Menard.

> (from Jorge Luis Borges, 'Pierre Menard, author of the *Quixote*')

By now the proposition that poets are tendentious readers, both of their own work and of the work of others, should be uncontroversial. What I want to do in this chapter and the next is to take a more sustained look at the operation *in allusive practice* of such tendentiousness than I have attempted heretofore – and, in doing so, to pursue the heuristic strategy of investing the term 'tendentiousness' with a positive rather than (as is more usual) a negative value. That is, rather than treating poetic tendentiousness primarily (as in much of chapter 3) as an epistemological hazard facing the would-be literary historian, I will seek to embrace it, even to celebrate it, as something *constitutive* of allusive writing and of the alluding poet's emplotment of his work in literary tradition.

1   Dialogue and tendentiousness

Recall, briefly, the terms of one of the correspondences discussed in chapter 1:

> hunc ego, fluminea deformis truncus harena
> qui iacet, agnosco ...   (Lucan 1.685–6)

>   ... iacet ingens litore truncus,
> avulsumque umeris caput et sine nomine corpus
>   (Virgil, *Aen.* 2.557–8)

As a reader of the Lucanian text, let me ask two overlapping questions about the dynamics of appropriation here – rhetorical questions in this instance, but destined for fuller exploration in a different case below (sections 2–4). The first can be felt to arise from, and to be complicated by, the details of my own earlier treatment. Which is the *master-text* in Lucan's allusive analogy? Is the Virgilian demise of Priam invoked as a standard by which to measure the Lucanian demise of Pompey, or does the Lucanian demise of Pompey become, through retrospective appropriation, a standard by which to measure the Virgilian demise of Priam? Second, what are the *limits* of Lucan's allusive analogy, whether over textual or over conceptual space? Is the Lucanian narrative of the fall of Pompey's Rome to be compared with the Virgilian narrative of the fall of Priam's Troy only in this one localized moment? Does the analogy colour our reading of *De Bello Civili* more systematically than this? If so, how systematically? Not a wholly idle question to ask in an epic whose other protagonist, Caesar, will later[1] visit the ruins of Troy and obliviously trample on the 'very' altar at which Virgil's Priam was slain (cf. chapter 3, section 4).

---

[1] Fully eight books later; but note that Caesar's visit to the Trojan ruins is juxtaposed in Book 9 with his receipt of the head of Pompey.

Modern scholarship on allusive relationships can be broadly divided, in fact, into studies of local contact (which tend to bracket out more systematic implications) and studies of systematic contact (which tend to bracket out details of local contact). In line with the Latinist's traditional preference for concrete and isolable effects over intertextual open-endedness of any kind (cf. chapter 2, section 1), purely local approaches have usually been predominant. Systematic approaches have been more intermittent, and where attempted, have tended to be unidirectional and (if I may so use this overworked term) non-dialogic. That is to say, if allusion is defined as a condensation of language and meaning in which one text (the alluding text) incorporates elements of another (the model text), *either* the alluding text *or* the model text is accorded the privilege of a systematic reading – but not both at the same time. Either the *incorporating* text is read systematically, with the incorporated text fragmented into discrete events 'alluded to', or the *incorporated* text is read systematically, with the incorporating text fragmented into discrete acts of allusive gesturing. The distinction can be illustrated most briefly by a caricature: the first formulation describes how Latinists once read all Virgilian allusions to Apollonius, the second how Hellenists once read all Apollonian allusions to Homer.

In the title of his fine book on Virgilian allusion to Homer (a more evenly balanced duo, for many, than the two allusive pairs just mentioned) Alessandro Barchiesi coins the term '*la traccia del modello*' to define the dynamics of textual incorporation. What makes this term such an attractive one is precisely its ability to negotiate – dialogically – between the two ways of reading just sketched. In Barchiesi's working metaphor, the Virgilian text incorporates *traccie* of the Homeric text. What are these *traccie*? From one point of view, just a scatter of Homeric *traces* in territory firmly constituted as Virgilian. From another point of view, however, a Homeric *track* or *trail*, which, once encountered in Virgilian territory, has the potential to lead the reader in directions determined no less by Homer than by Virgil.[2]

As (modern) readers of Roman poetry, why, in a given case of allusive incorporation, do we tend to privilege only one of the texts involved with

---

[2] Barchiesi's (1984) title is rendered by Fowler (1991), 90, as 'the *trace/trail/track* of the model'.

a systematic reading, while reading the other[3] 'fragmentarily'? Here are two reasons, to be followed almost immediately by a third. First, one of the texts is – quite literally – a fragment, so that a fully dialogic approach is already precluded by the accidents of survival. Second, one of the texts is felt to be less important, less 'good', less canonical than the other (like Apollonius in the caricature diptych above, or as in the older modern accounts of Neronian or Flavian allusion to Augustan poetry invoked in chapter 3): i.e. one of the two texts is felt to be insufficiently interesting to merit systematic reading, or to have so little compositional integrity of its own as to be incapable of responding to systematic reading.

As an excuse for the evolution of a 'non-dialogic' poetics of allusion, the first of these reasons is perhaps the more honourable one. Indeed this explanation may have some force even in cases in which fragmentary survival is not an issue. Probably because of the genesis of Latin literary studies in nineteenth-century traditions of *Quellenforschung*, a great deal of the foundational work on allusion in Roman poetry has involved the study and elucidation of models which (for us) survive only in fragments: e.g. Pasquali's seminal 'Arte allusiva', for all that it constructs itself as something entirely different from old-style source-hunting,[4] concentrates precisely on such cases, in which the incorporating text is fully extant, but the incorporated text available to the modern interpreter only in fragments. Such an emphasis may be habit-forming: hence, perhaps, the deep-seated predisposition among Latinists to 'fragment' even non-fragmentary texts in the interpretation of allusive relationships.[5]

But let me now propose a third, more universal explanation, which encompasses the other two without, however, entirely displacing or superseding them. A case can be made that full dialogue is always an unattainable ideal – that it is ultimately *impossible*, at any given moment in any study of allusive incorporation, *not* to privilege one of two texts

---

[3] For the economy of the present argument I envisage a relationship between just *two* texts, one incorporating and one incorporated. In what follows, however, multiple simultaneous incorporation will not be ignored.

[4] Pasquali (1951), 11 'rispondo: Io non cerco, io non ho mai cercato le fonti di una poesia'.

[5] Recent work by classicists on questions of reception is notably alive to negotiations of various kinds between the fragmentary and the 'fragmentary': cf. Rosenmeyer (1991) on Simonides' Danae fragment; Connors (1998), 8–11, on Petronius' *Satyricon*.

involved over the other. On this explanation, such a privileging is *required* by the minimal linearity of response necessary to define reading as reading. We can point to particular distortions or impoverishments caused by a failure to read one of the two texts systematically; but in the final analysis a systematic reading of one text will always preclude a systematic reading of the other. Such an imbalance does not necessarily imply an act of wilful devaluation. A reading of Virgil which 'fragments' the Homeric model into discrete events 'alluded to' may reflect nothing more (and nothing less) than a basic interpretative imperative felt by the Virgilian reader to 'freeze' Homer, to *hold him still* for a moment so that he can be contemplated from a Virgilian point of view.[6] In this way, *any* reading of a relationship between an incorporating text and an incorporated text will always be a tendentious reading – which is by no means to limit the rich possibilities for discussion of degrees and kinds of tendentiousness, of greater and lesser failures to achieve dialogue.

'Any reading': it is time to bring things back, as promised, to the first reader of any instance of allusive incorporation, a reader by no means exempt from this inevitability of tendentiousness: the alluding poet himself. An allusion is always an expression of partiality; by definition no account of an allusive intervention in poetic discourse can proceed far without accepting – more strictly, without constructing[7] – the alluding poet as focalizer of that account, however conditionally. Unlike in chapters 1–3, I shall allow the agenda of the present chapter to shape and adapt itself to an extended close reading of a single sustained pattern of allusion: not because a (neo-) new-critical privileging of arguments particular to one allusive event offers more unmediated access to interpretative truth, but because it may better dramatize some dynamics of interpretative mediation. I have selected a case-study in which, not only are the links between the related texts especially clear and pronounced, but the *processes* of intertextual negotiation are unusually heightened and foregrounded.[8] My incorporating text is a segment of Ovid's *Metamorphoses*, 13.623–14.582; my incorporated text is

---

[6] For this formulation I am indebted to a conversation with Richard Thomas – to add to my many debts to his articles.

[7] Cf. chapter 2, section 5.

[8] For the identification of *symptoms* of intertextual process polemically privileged over the identification of actual intertexts, cf. the reading programme of Michael Riffaterre, as discussed by Worton and Still (1990), 26–7.

Virgil's *Aeneid*. Not a vignette from the *Aeneid*, not an episode from the *Aeneid*, but the *Aeneid* in its entirety. This *tour de force* of intertextual repetition and change (already something of a *locus classicus* for modern critics of Roman poetry) will be as good a laboratory as any in which to explore some of the highways and by-ways of allusive tendentiousness.

2   Ovid's *Aeneid* (and Virgil's *Metamorphoses*)

Ovid's *Metamorphoses* is the first major Roman epic to be written in the wake of the *Aeneid*, and, perhaps, the least anxious about its own post-Virgilian status. Not that the *Metamorphoses* simply ignores the *Aeneid*, as it surely could, being such a different kind of epic. No. Again and again in the rich catalogue of episodes which makes up the poem's version of universal history, stories, characters and situations come up which, although not themselves Virgilian, evoke and engage with Virgilian types – notably, for example, in the Theban cycle in *Metamorphoses* 3 and 4, as suggestively analysed by Philip Hardie.[9] But more than twelve and a half books into the poem, at a point where the *Metamorphoses* has just overtaken the *Aeneid* in length, Ovid offers something more directly Virgilian. Embracing the logic of a claim to mythic and chronological comprehensiveness, he brings his poem from Troy to Italy in the most obvious and yet most audacious way possible: by annexing the whole *Aeneid* to the *Metamorphoses*. In a miracle of summarizing and miniaturization, Virgil's classic epic of almost 10,000 lines becomes two contiguous part-books of Ovid's epic (totalling about 1,000 lines) – a sort of super-episode.

Right from the outset there are elements of paradox and tendentiousness in this move. The position might reasonably be held that 'Ovid's *Aeneid*' – the label has been standard for some years now – is in some ways the *least* Virgilian thing he ever wrote. If an extended Ovidian treatment of the death of Dido is sought, it can be found – in *Heroides* 7. A response in the *Metamorphoses* to the Turnus/Aeneas conflict? Certainly – in the Virgilian types of the Achelous/Hercules fight in *Metamorphoses* 9, or of Phineus/Perseus in *Metamorphoses* 5. But in the narrative of *Metamorphoses* 13–14, where one might expect to find them,

---

[9] Hardie (1990), subtitled 'The first "Anti-*Aeneid*"?'.

these Virgilian high-points are firmly in the background. Here, in fact, is
the entire Dido episode in Ovid's *Aeneid* (14.77–81):

> . . . Libycas vento referuntur ad oras.
> excipit Aenean illic animoque domoque
> non bene discidium Phrygii latura mariti
> Sidonis, inque pyra sacri sub imagine facta
> incubuit ferro deceptaque decipit omnes

> The wind bore them back to the Libyan coast. There the Sidonian
> queen welcomed Aeneas in heart and home, destined ill to bear the
> parting from her Phrygian husband: on a pyre, built under pretence
> of holy rites, she fell upon his sword and, herself deceived, deceived
> all.

So much for Carthage: one sixth of Virgil's *Aeneid*, one two-hundredth
of Ovid's *Aeneid*.

If Ovid 'backgrounds' major players such as Dido and Turnus, what
does he foreground? No prizes for guessing the answer: *Virgilian stories
of metamorphosis*. Major players in *this* version of the Trojan migration
epic include the magician-goddess Circe, an agent of transformation
(one five-hundredth of Virgil's *Aeneid*, but a full quarter of Ovid's
Aeneid), and the part-woman part-monster Scylla, available for con-
strual as a victim of transformation (one four-hundredth of Virgil's
Aeneid, but a full fifth of Ovid's *Aeneid*). And hidden in those bare
statistics is the further emphasis which Ovid gives to these two bit-
players in the *Aeneid* by bringing them together into one story: in this
version it is actually Circe who inflicts metamorphic change on Scylla.
The question is this: how should the dynamics be interpreted here,
between incorporating Ovidian and incorporated Virgilian text?

To repeat a ploy from chapter 3, section 4, let me summon up a typical
reader of the *Metamorphoses* from a mere two decades ago, when it was
a widespread article of faith among Latinists that the perfection of the
Aeneid had effectively imposed closure upon the history of Roman epic,
and that any subsequent Roman poet with more than an ounce of sense
recognized Virgil's poem to be by its very nature *inimitable*: such a reader
would most likely argue that Ovid, faced with the high moral seriousness
of the *Aeneid*, has a failure of nerve and runs away from the centre of
Virgil's poem, pilfering *en route* such scraps as can be incorporated –

fragmentarily – into his own metamorphic project.[10] Being a reader of the *Metamorphoses* in the mid-1990s, when the recanonization of Ovid has raised his status to something not far short of institutional equality with Virgil for the first time since the eighteenth century,[11] I myself am naturally inclined to envisage a stronger Ovidian reading of the *Aeneid* than this. A reading of *Met.* 13.623–14.582 positioned some 197 decades after its production and my own reading positioned some 199 decades on can agree up to a point on an objective description of what Ovid is doing. He tracks the narrative line of the *Aeneid* closely; but wherever Virgil is elaborate, Ovid is brief, and wherever Virgil is brief, Ovid elaborates . . . and generally elaborates in such a way as to develop the characteristic themes of his own epic, not those of Virgil's. My mid-1990s 'spin' on this would be that Ovid is engaged in a tendentious poetic appropriation of his predecessor – a kind of bid for teleological control. Rather than construct himself as an epigonal reader of the *Aeneid*, Ovid is constructing Virgil as a hesitant precursor of the *Metamorphoses*. There is a *Metamorphoses* latent in the *Aeneid*, Ovid's treatment tells us: in Circe and in the biform Scylla, as also in the transformation of Aeneas' ships into nymphs and in the transformation of Diomedes' companions into birds. But in Virgil these myths are fragmented, scattered, unresolved: not until Ovid's own poem are they gathered into perfection and system.[12]

[10] In essence, such a characterization can embrace even a treatment as sympathetic as Galinsky (1975): 224 '[Ovid] was not concerned with an *aemulatio* of Vergil's masterpiece, which he rightly recognized to be inimitable'; cf. 220 'Ovid *wisely* decided not to compete with Vergil's lengthy and dramatic account of Aeneas' flight from Troy' (emph. mine). Especially at Cambridge (variables are geographical as well as chronological), it was E.J. Kenney who freed the *Metamorphoses* from such lingering Virgiliocentrism for a new generation of critics.

[11] . . . and when readings of the *Aeneid* itself envisage no literary historical 'closure' without 'continuation': Hardie (1993), 1–18.

[12] Aeneas' ships: *Aen.* 9.77–122, *Met.* 14.530–65. Diomedes' companions: n.30 below. Interesting here is the long-standing unease occasioned by the metamorphic ships in the critical tradition on Virgil's *Aeneid*. Serv. *Aen.* 9.81 *figmentum hoc licet poeticum sit, tamen quia exemplo caret, notatur a criticis: unde longo prooemio excusatur* 'granted that this is a poetic fiction, yet because it lacks a precedent, it attracts critical censure: whence Virgil justifies it with a long preamble'. Cf. R.D. Williams (1973) on *Aen.* 9.77: 'This is the most incongruous episode in the whole *Aeneid*, and has been censured by the critics from the time of Servius onwards . . . Page finds the subject "somewhat ludicrous", and Heyne says it is easy to censure it as "absurdam

Hence the parenthetic 'Virgil's *Metamorphoses*' added to 'Ovid's *Aeneid*' in the present section's title, a supplement which seeks to extend the terms of the (inevitably unbalanced) dialogue between *Metamorphoses* and *Aeneid* here at *Met.* 13.623–14.582. Is this super-episode a tale of centrifugal Ovidian response to the *Aeneid*, or is it a tale of centripetal Virgilian anticipation of the *Metamorphoses*? The question has arisen from an awareness of shifting positionalities among Ovid's modern readers, each involving claims about Ovid's own position; and that very awareness of the importance of positionality within such a discussion should make us wary of any easy or definitive response.[13]

3   Epic repetition: remakes, sequels, doubles

To argue for bold reconfigurations of the Virgilian model in *Metamorphoses* 13–14 is one way of tackling this celebrated nexus. Still, it is important to remember that 'Ovid's *Aeneid*' owes its nickname not to any striking points of divergence from Virgil's *Aeneid*, but to its striking points of coincidence. Let us continue this case-study in allusive tendentiousness by examining some of the moments at which Ovid's *Aeneid* looks *most like* Virgil's. We shall find that the dynamics of incorporation become more complicated, not less so, the closer Ovid comes to direct replication of his predecessor's narrative moves.

Consider first the juncture in *Metamorphoses* 14 at which Aeneas emerges from the underworld and moves on from Cumae to his next port of call (14.154–7):

---

et epica gravitate indignam [unsuited to the dignity of epic]". *The story is told in Ov. Met. 14.530f., where it easily and naturally belongs.*' (tr. and emph. mine). Cf. now the revaluation of Fantham (1990), esp. 103.

[13] Other revisionist accounts of *Met.* 13.623–14.582 as a 'strong' Ovidian reading of the *Aeneid*: Solodow (1988), 136–56, esp. 142; Tissol (1993). Tissol (his n.4) denies the strength of Solodow's Ovid, relegating him to the same 'weak' category as Galinsky's – a move which dramatizes the difficulty of separating ancient poetic from modern critical agendas in mapping out this story of 'stronger than thou'. Hardie (1992), esp. 62–9, further complicates the dynamics of the question by arguing that the *Aeneid* was a metamorphic poem – and profoundly so – *even before* Ovid tendentiously constructed it as such.

talia convexum per iter memorante Sibylla
sedibus Euboicam Stygiis emergit in urbem
Troius Aeneas sacrisque ex more litatis
litora adit nondum nutricis habentia nomen

While thus along the arching way the Sibyl tells her tale, Trojan
Aeneas emerges from the Stygian abodes into the Euboean city. After
due sacrifices here, he next approaches the shores that do not yet bear
his nurse's name.

In this passage Ovid is following the narrative line of the *Aeneid* very
closely indeed. Closely, but by no means inertly. The verse emphasized
above has about it the air of an editorial comment: here is the Virgilian
'original' (*Aen.* 6.897–901):

his ibi tum natum Anchises unaque Sibyllam
prosequitur dictis portaque emittit eburna:
ille viam secat ad naves sociosque revisit.
tum se ad Caietae recto fert limite portum.
ancora de prora iacitur; stant litore puppes

There then Anchises escorts his son and the Sibyl with these words,
and sends them out by the ivory gate: Aeneas cuts a path to the ships
and back to his friends. Then he steers a straight course for the port of
Caieta. The anchor is thrown from the prow; the ships rest upon the
shore.

Ovid is not engaging at this point with any random moment in the
Aeneid; these are the closing lines of Book 6, the closing lines of the first,
'Odyssean' half of the epic (more on *that* label shortly). Virgil's Aeneas
approaches the harbour of Caieta, so named, as Ovid indicates with his
'gloss' on *Aen.* 6.900, for the hero's dead nurse, who is buried there.
However, as Ovid's 'gloss' also indicates, Virgil has used the name
prematurely. As Aeneas' ship approaches the shore, his nurse is not yet
buried there, so that the shore is not yet called Caieta: *nondum nutricis
habentia nomen*. Virgil's next book, and the second half of the *Aeneid*,
opens by redressing the situation (*Aen.* 7.1–7):

tu quoque litoribus nostris, Aeneia nutrix,
aeternam moriens famam, Caieta, dedisti;
et nunc servat honos sedem tuus, ossaque nomen

Hesperia in magna, si qua est ea gloria, signat.
at pius exsequiis Aeneas rite solutis,
aggere composito tumuli, postquam alta quierunt
aequora, tendit iter velis portumque relinquit

You too, Caieta, nurse of Aeneas, have given eternal fame to our shores by your death; the honour paid you still guards your resting-place, and your name marks your bones in great Hesperia, if that renown be anything. Now pious Aeneas duly discharged the funeral rites, and raised the mound of the tomb; then, when the high seas have become calm, he sets sail and leaves the port.

Now of course Virgil, and Ovid no less, are entirely familiar with the figure of prolepsis.[14] What Ovid's mock-pedantic correction is really designed to do, I think, is to show his enjoyment of a very (dare I say it?) Ovidian moment in his predecessor. The *Metamorphoses* is a poem in which boundaries between books tend to be of less consequence than boundaries between episodes: thus (for instance) within 'Ovid's *Aeneid*', itself a super-episode spanning two contiguous part-books, the actual division between *Metamorphoses* 13 and 14 is straddled by the c.150-line tale of Scylla and Glaucus. The *Aeneid*, in contrast, generally shows profound respect for the book as a structural unit – except right here at the midpoint of the epic, where Virgil virtuosically bridges the most important structural divide in his poem with a minor, apparently inconsequential episode; and does so in such a way that the reader is narratologically impelled across the book-divide by the need to fill out the prolepsis which has prematurely named a shore for a woman whose death and burial there have yet to be told.[15] The second, 'Iliadic' half of the *Aeneid* will begin with a formal reinvocation of the Muse . . . but 37 lines *into* Book 7, not in the conventional initial position which the Caietan bridge-narrative has usurped.[16]

[14] . . . and Servius too, whose pedantic note on *Aen.* 6.900 is exactly anticipated by Ovid's mock-pedantry: *a persona poetae prolepsis: nam Caieta nondum dicebatur.*

[15] Jeffrey Wills (in an oral footnote to a discussion of *Aen.* 6.901 forthcoming in *MD*) wonders about the shore itself as a figure for the divide. *Aen.* 6.901 *litore*, 7.1 *litoribus*: the structural 'shores' of Virgil's poem?

[16] The invocation of Erato at *Aen.* 7.37–44 famously echoes the invocation of Erato at the (true) midpoint of Apollonius' *Argonautica*: 3.1–5. Cf. Fowler (1989), 94–5, noting too a telling Homeric precedent for the 'delayed' midpoint of the *Aeneid* in the mismatch between the end of the hero's voyage and the (editorial) division between the two 12-book halves of the *Odyssey*.

This is what Ovid is concerned to salute. Nor has he yet finished playing his own narratological game with Caieta. Like Virgil's prolepsis, Ovid's *nondum* sets up a narrative expectation; and Ovid duly fulfils it. Here is his 'completion' of the Caieta story (*Met.* 14.441–5):

> . . . urnaque Aeneia nutrix
> condita marmoreo tumulo breve carmen habebat:
> 'hic me Caietam notae pietatis alumnus
> ereptam Argolico quo debuit igne cremavit.'
> solvitur herboso religatus ab aggere funis

And the nurse of Aeneas, laid in an urn, had this brief inscription on her marble tomb: 'Here me, Caieta, rescued from Argive fire, my nursling of well-known piety burned on a fitting pyre.' The fastened rope is loosed from the grassy mound . . .

Caieta is cremated by her *notae pietatis alumnus* (the adjective perhaps 'annotates' the inevitable *at pius . . . . Aeneas* found at the equivalent moment in the Virgilian model-passage, *Aen.* 7.5). And so Aeneas proceeds onward in his journey, his final act being (in 445) to cast off the ship's rope from an *agger*, a mound (not, presumably, from Caieta's burial-mound itself, though it is weirdly hard to resist the lexical pull of the equivalent (?) *agger* in *Aen.* 7.6[17]). But before following him, I have yet to note something remarkable, disguised in my exposition above. Like Virgil's *Aeneid*, Ovid's presents the Caieta vignette in two parts. But whereas in Virgil the two parts are adjacent, positioned on each side of his poem's median division so as to be separated only by the physical change in book-roll, in Ovid they are separated by a substantial narrative interposition (*Met.* 14.158–440). Where Virgil had sought to close the *Aeneid*'s most obvious structural break with a virtuoso narrative bridge, Ovid, with equal virtuosity, forces back open the gap between *Aeneid* 6 and 7, and inserts almost 300 lines of poetry into it

---

[17] Is this fleeting idea abetted by something subliminally funereal in the very juxtaposition *aggere funis*? For ancient etymologizing associations between *funis* 'rope' and *funus* 'funeral' see Maltby (1991) s.v. *funus*, along with McKeown (1987–), I, 60 on Ov. *Am.* 2.11.23; and with the phrase *solvitur . . . funis* (*Met.* 14.445) compare, again subliminally, Virgil's *exsequiis . . . solutis* (*Aen.* 7.5). These suggestions complicate the philologically tight allusive correspondence (noted since Kroll (1924), 172) between *Met.* 14.445 and a later Virgilian verse associated with Aeneas' next landfall, *Aen.* 7.106. My thanks to Laura Baldwin for help in pursuing these reverberations.

(three tenths of his total remake, to revert to the statistical approach). In other words, not only does Ovid's *nondum* stall the narrative acceleration effected by Virgil's prolepsis, but that delay is immediately compounded by a massive Ovidian 'interpolation' between *Met.* 14.157 and 441.

The contents of this interpolation yield our next case of mannered allusive repetition. What occupies *Met.* 14.158–440 is Ovid's well-known twofold response (a remake-with-sequel, followed by a mythic double) to one particular highly charged episode in the third book of Virgil's *Aeneid*.[18] In *Aen.* 3.590–691 Virgil had introduced his voyaging Trojans to Achaemenides, a crewman inadvertently left behind in the land of the Cyclopes by Ulysses, and now encountered there by Aeneas and his men. This is the only time in Virgil's epic that the world of the *Odyssey* and the world of the *Aeneid*, so intimately connected at the level of the narrative intertext, are permitted to come together openly at the level of narrated action. In general, as Barchiesi has noted, Virgil fastidiously avoids the possibility, logically available in the mythic chronology, of having the voyaging Aeneas actually bump into his Homeric prototype at some port of call around the Mediterranean.[19] However the idea is too good for Virgil to renounce completely: hence the invention of the marooned Achaemenides, who is picked up by Aeneas' fleet and duly offers his rescuers a post-Homeric remake (more exactly: part remake, part sequel) of the Cyclops episode recounted to the Phaeacians by Ulysses in *Odyssey* 9.

It is this episode to which Ovid offers a twofold answer in the gap which he has opened up at Caieta, right at the half-way point of the *Aeneid*. For whom should Ovid's Trojans meet at this later port on their journey but *another* drop-out from Ulysses' crew, a man called Macareus (an Ovidian invention to match Virgil's)? Naturally he and Achaemenides, who is 'still' travelling with the Trojan fleet, are delighted to see each other; and what they do, of course, is swap stories. Achaemenides offers a remake-with-sequel of the post-Homeric remake-with-sequel of the Cyclops episode which he (i.e. 'he') had already offered in Virgil's *Aeneid*, repeating some parts of the story and adding others (many of them Homeric) not covered before. And Macareus, who (as he himself reveals) had left his shipmates directly after their long year

---

[18] Cf. most recently Esposito (1994), 11–36, with bibl.   [19] Barchiesi (1986), 88–9.

on the island of Circe, responds by filling in Achaemenides on the highlights of the Odyssean voyage from Aeolus' abode to Circe's, in an embellished remake[20] of what Ulysses had recounted to the Phaeacians in the following, tenth book of Homer's epic.[21]

Macareus, then, is an Ovidian mythic double of Virgil's Achaemenides.[22] In effect Ovid here offers 'Achaemenides II' not once but twice; and the full measure of this culminating event of allusive incorporation can now be seen. By thus privileging and responding to the *Aeneid*'s Achaemenides episode, Ovid's *Aeneid* identifies Virgil's *Aeneid* as its precursor in the art of the tendentious remake – an art represented, of course, by Ovid's *Aeneid* itself *in toto*. The redoubling of (meta-) epic repetition almost defies description: Ovid thematizes his intertextual dialogue with his epic predecessor – and here, if anywhere, 'dialogue' is the *mot juste* – by putting an Odyssean stray of his own into conversation with the Odyssean stray through whom Virgil had thematized *his* intertextual dialogue with *his* epic predecessor. Amid such appropriations and reappropriations, it becomes hard to know at any given juncture whether *we* are responding to a Virgilian Ovid, a Homeric Virgil, or a Homeric Ovid . . . or indeed (to recall the paradoxes of section 2) to an Ovidian Virgil, a Virgilian Homer, or an Ovidian Homer.

[20] A different kind of account of Ovid's *Aeneid* could dwell much more fully on such 'embellishments' (here, esp. the enclosed tale of Picus and Canens), and on the many allusive strands which complicate and compete with the inter-epic relationships privileged in my account: see esp. Myers (1994), 98–113. A further rich source of complication not explored here is the *intra*textual 'doubling' of the Cyclops and Circe, whose roles in the Achaemenides–Macareus complex ask to be read against their roles in the Galatea–Scylla complex earlier in Ovid's *Aeneid*.

[21] Ovid's remake of Homer's Circe episode also answers the *Aeneid* in that Virgil had literally skirted the same narratological possibility when the Trojans passed within ear-shot of Circe's shores at *Aen.* 7.10–24 (directly after their departure from Caieta; cf. *Met.* 14.446–7).

[22] Ovid may underline Macareus' status as an *ad hoc* coinage by making him the etymological antonym of Achaemenides, rooted in 'happiness' rather than in 'pain' – unless his name rather alludes (through a more oblique antonymy) to Virgil's initial description of the person of Achaemenides as *macie confecta suprema* (*Aen.* 3.590, quoted below). Such etymological forcing of the (Persian!) name Achaemenides may be a tendentious rewrite of an equally forced Virgilian etymology: for the idea that Achaemenides is so named in the *Aeneid* to hint at his status as a generic Greek (cf. 3.594 *at cetera Graius*), cf. O'Hara (1996), 147, with bibl.

It is worth dwelling for a moment on the first appearance(s) of the palimpsestic Achaemenides. A primitivized mess when Virgil's Trojans rescue him from the land of the Cyclopes (*Aen.* 3.590–4),

> cum subito e silvis macie confecta suprema
> ignoti nova forma viri miserandaque cultu
> procedit supplexque manus ad litora tendit.
> respicimus. dira illuvies immissaque barba,
> *consertum tegimen spinis . . .*

When suddenly a strange figure of a man unknown, emaciated to the last degree, and pitiable in aspect, comes forth from the woods and stretches out his hands in supplication towards the shore. We look back: he was in horrid filth, his beard unkempt, his garments pinned with thorns

Achaemenides has had a good brush-up and shave by the time he is re-encountered in Ovid's poem (*Met.* 14.165–6):

> . . . iam non hirsutus amictu,
> iam suus et *spinis conserto tegmine nullis*

No longer roughly clad, now his own man, his garments no longer pinned with thorns . . .

When read as a reflexive annotation (in the manner of Ariadne's Contean *memini*), *iam non* can nicely catch two kinds of chronology here, not just mythological but also literary historical: 'now' as opposed to how he was back in the land of the Cyclopes; but also 'now' as opposed to how he was back in the text of Virgil's *Aeneid* . . . where, in turn, we may be tempted to read his extreme decay (*macie . . . suprema*) as itself an index of the passage of time not just since the departure of Ulysses' ship but also, metapoetically, since the composition of Homer's *Odyssey*. Equally suggestive in the Ovidian passage is *iam suus*, 'now his own man'. In the case of an intertextual figure like Achaemenides, such an affirmation of identity cannot but read tendentiously. Does Ovid thus imply that Achaemenides was a mere cipher in Virgil, and has become a fully achieved character only in the *Metamorphoses*? Or that the *Metamorphoses* 'restores' Achaemenides to a (lost) original, Homeric state? How can *any* character be said fully to belong to himself in this intertextual world? On any such metapoetic construction,[23] Ovid's *suus* responds to and 'caps' Virgil's *ignoti nova forma viri*, which is simultaneously an arch denial of Achaemenides' status as a derivative character,[24] and a literally true designation of a particular Odyssean crewman who never achieved named individuality back in Homer's epic.[25]

Appropriately enough, the first word uttered by Ovid's Achaemenides, just below, is '*iterum*', as he prays that he may be consigned 'again' to the Cyclops if his gratitude to Aeneas should ever fade (*Met.* 14.167–71).[26] His second word is '*Polyphemon*'; and repetitious action involving Polyphemus is precisely what dominates his tale told to Macareus at *Met.* 14.167–222. Thus, in recalling how he was stranded by the departure of Ulysses, he reports a speech in which the Cyclops, now blind and blundering about Mount Etna, looks to the future to find some gastronomic redress for the past (*Met.* 14.192–7):

> atque ait: 'o si quis referat mihi casus Ulixem
> aut aliquem e sociis, in quem mea saeviat ira,
> viscera cuius edam, cuius viventia dextra
> membra mea laniem, cuius mihi sanguis inundet
> guttur *et elisi trepident sub dentibus artus*,
> quam nullum aut leve sit damnum mihi lucis ademptae!'

Said he: 'Oh, that some chance would bring Ulysses back to me, or some one of his friends, against whom my rage might vent itself, whose guts I might devour, whose living members I might rend with

---

[23] A narratologist might frame the matter thus: *suus* is reflexive not just in the syntax of the sentence but also in the 'syntax' of the narrative intertext. *Suus* functions more straightforwardly in overt rhetorical discussions of allusive appropriation: e.g. Sen. *Contr.* 7.1.27 *Varro quem voluit sensum optime explicuit, Ovidius in illius versu suum sensum invenit* 'Varro developed the idea he wanted excellently, while Ovid found in Varro's verse an idea of his own.'

[24] An archness perhaps compounded in the 'backward look' bestowed upon Achaemenides by the Virgilian sailors just below (3.593 *respicimus*): cf. *OLD* s.v. *respicio* 1, with 5, along with Connors (1998), 91, on an analogous instance at Petr. 89.35.

[25] Patricia Rosenmeyer, Jeffrey Wills and Denis Feeney all had a hand in these last two sentences.

[26] *iterum* in a context of reflexive annotation: cf. *Fast.* 3.471–2 (quoted in chapter 1, section 1) with Conte (1986), 61–2.

my hand, whose blood might flood my throat, and whose mangled limbs might tremble under my teeth! How nothing then, how trifling, would be the loss of my stolen sight!'

With the italicized clause compare a clause in *Virgil*'s Achaemenides episode, noting in passing how the Ovidian *trepident* assonantally dovetails the Virgilian *tepidi* and *tremerent* (*Aen.* 3.626–7):

> . . . vidi atro cum membra fluentia tabo
> manderet *et tepidi tremerent sub dentibus artus*

I saw, when he chewed their members flowing with black gore, and their warm limbs twitched under his teeth . . .

In these words Virgil's Achaemenides is recounting the ingestion of his shipmates' limbs by the (previous) Cyclops. Thus Ovid's Cyclops, as quoted by the *new* Achaemenides, remakes in his anticipation of a future banquet the very words in which his (or rather 'his') earlier banquet had been described by the previous Achaemenides. The Cyclops' vengeful wish for the future is enacted at the level of intertextual quotation as a repeat of a specifically Virgilian past – which had itself fused a character's 'lived' memory with a poetic memory of a (doubled!) event in Homer's *Odyssey* (9.289–91, 311).[27] Lest that all seem too simple, Ovid goes on to double his remake of *Aen.* 3.623–7 by having *his* Achaemenides recount his own 'lived' memory of the Virgilian scene just allusively evoked in his quotation of the Cyclops (*Met.* 14.204–5 *mentique haerebat imago / temporis illius, quo vidi . . .* 'and the picture stuck in my mind of that time, when I saw . . .') – a cue for still more allusions to Virgil and to Homer.

For poets who handle mythological themes, occasions for negotiation between the time-frames of the narrated world and the time-frames of their own poetic traditions will tend to arise again and again. Ovid has a rare appetite for reflexively highlighting these moments of intersection between different temporal realities; but such intersections will be part of one's experience of reading *any* mythological text within a strongly unified literary system like that of Greco-Roman epic – whether a given

---

[27] Another twist: the Cyclops' vengeful speech at *Met.* 14.192–7 also reiterates his earlier (and 'earlier') vengeful speech at *Od.* 9.456–60: Baldo (1986), 121.

poet seeks them out actively or not. Take the lost Trojan war epic by Ovid's contemporary Macer (Ovid, *Am.* 2.18.1):

> carmen *ad iratum* dum tu perducis *Achillem*

> While you take your poem down to the wrath of Achilles . . .

Not a single word of Macer's poem survives. Nonetheless, there is a sense in which we know quite well how to read it: viz as a 'prequel' to Homer's *Iliad*, in the mode which Barchiesi has dubbed 'future reflexive'.[28]

For one last allusive vignette in Ovid's *Aeneid*, I move to the war in Italy. Among the Virgilian kings and leaders refashioned here, Ovid gives the largest coverage not to Turnus, not to Evander (who receives a single line), but to Diomedes – to whom, as in Virgil's *Aeneid*, the Latins send envoys unsuccessfully seeking military help against the Trojans. Why Diomedes? This, remember, is the Greek hero who had notoriously wounded the goddess Aphrodite in Book 5 of Homer's *Iliad*, while trying to prevent her from rescuing Aeneas, whom he, Diomedes, had been about to crush in combat: he is, then, a Homeric hero imported for a Virgilian sequel in which he declines ever to tangle with Aeneas or his divine mother again. Hence Ovid's interest. All the martial encounters in the second half of Virgil's *Aeneid* involve some allusive doubling of Iliadic battle action; but only Diomedes offers the prospect of an actual rematch.[29] In remaking Diomedes, then, Ovid's *Aeneid* remakes Virgil's so-called '*Iliad*' at its most self-consciously Homeric.

In Ovid's poem, as in Virgil's, Diomedes tells the Latin envoys the tale of the metamorphosis of his companions into birds, a misadventure which occupies four lines in Virgil but six times that in Ovid.[30] In that

---

[28] Barchiesi (1993) with (1986); cf. Goldhill's 'back to the future' at (1991), 284 with 249–50 (on the *Theocritean* Cyclops and Homer). On 'prequels' cf. Hinds (1993), 40; also chapter 3, section 5 above on Stat. *Ach.* 1.20–94. Macer may have followed up his '*Antehomerica*' with a later '*Posthomerica*': see Ov. *Pont.* 2.10.13–14 with McKeown's (forthcoming) intro. n. on *Am.* 2.18.

[29] On the prospect declined, and on the Turnus of the *Aeneid*'s final duel as an imperfect mythic double of the missing Diomedes, see Quint (1989), 35–43, within a notable study of the ideology of Virgilian repetition; also Lyne (1987), 132–5, esp. 133 on *Aen.* 1.94–101.

[30] *Aen.* 11.271–4, *Met.* 14.484–509. On the literary genealogy of Ovid's embellishments see Myers (1994), 102–4 (with my n.20 above).

sense Diomedes is one of those Virgilian characters who belong more organically in the *Metamorphoses* than in the *Aeneid*; but my interest for the present discussion is in something earlier in his speech. In both epics Diomedes begins with an account of his and his fellow-Greeks' voyage home from Troy, culminating in the disastrous sea-storm off the Euboean promontory of Caphereus. The Ovidian Diomedes then goes on to describe a *further* period of wandering when he is driven out of his homeland . . . and at this point, oddly enough, his story starts to sound distinctly like the story, not of Virgil's Diomedes (who at *Aen.* 11.269–70 'backgrounds' this phase of his wandering), but of Virgil's Aeneas (*Met.* 14.476–9):[31]

> . . . patriis sed rursus ab agris
> pellor, et antiquo memores de vulnere poenas
> exigit alma Venus, tantosque per alta labores
> aequora sustinui, tantos terrestribus armis

> But again I was driven out of my native country, and fostering Venus now exacted the penalty, still mindful, for her former wound. Such great toils did I endure on the high seas, such great toils in war on land
> . . .

Substitute Juno's mindful anger for Venus', and what we have here is a near-double of the opening five lines of Virgil's *Aeneid*. As Diomedes completes his sentence the allusive analogy becomes even more interesting:

> ut mihi felices sint illi saepe vocati,
> quos communis hiems importunusque Caphereus
> mersit aquis, vellemque horum pars una fuissem

> . . . that often did I call fortunate those whom the shared storm and ruthless Caphereus drowned beneath the waves; and I wished that I had been one of them.

If Diomedes was shadowing the *incipit* lines of the *Aeneid* in 476–9, here in 480–2 he shadows Aeneas' own first speech in the Virgilian epic (*Aen.* 1.94–101):

---

[31] So too independently Margaret Musgrove, in a fine paper on Diomedes in Virgil and Ovid which I have seen in typescript.

talia voce refert: 'o terque quaterque beati,
quis ante ora patrum Troiae sub moenibus altis
contigit oppetere! o Danaum fortissime gentis
Tydide! mene Iliacis occumbere campis
non potuisse tuaque animam hanc effundere dextra,
saevus ubi Aeacidae telo iacet Hector, ubi ingens
Sarpedon, ubi tot Simois correpta sub undis
scuta virum galeasque et fortia corpora volvit!'

He thus cries out: 'O thrice and four times blessed those whose
fortune it was to die before their fathers' eyes, beneath the high walls
of Troy! O you, bravest of the Greeks, son of Tydeus, why could I not
have fallen on the Trojan plains, and poured out my soul by your
right hand? – where fierce Hector lies low beneath the spear of
Achilles; where mighty Sarpedon lies; where Simois has seized and
sweeps beneath its waters so many shields and helmets and bodies of
brave warriors!'

No verbal correspondences for the concordance-bound critic to mark;
but the allusion is indubitable. Diomedes' death-wish both repeats and
caps Aeneas'. Aeneas, in the middle of a post-Trojan shipwreck, envies
those of his compatriots who had died at Troy; Diomedes, in the middle
of a further phase of wandering, envies those of his compatriots who had
died in the middle of a post-Trojan shipwreck.[32]

Finally, as if to complete the allusive embrace of the *Aeneid*'s opening
columns, the very *next* lines of Diomedes' speech (*Met.* 14.483–4)

ultima iam passi comites belloque fretoque
deficiunt *finemque rogant* erroris . . .

My companions, having now endured the utmost in war and on sea,
became disheartened and pleaded for an end to wandering

pick up the opening of Aeneas' *second* speech in Virgil (*Aen.* 1.198–9):

'o socii (neque enim ignari sumus ante malorum),
o passi graviora, dabit deus his quoque *finem*'

---

[32] Aeneas' death-wish is of course already Odyssean (*Od.* 5.306–12); Diomedes' owes
an ancillary debt to *Aen.* 11.255–60.

'O comrades, who have endured worse (for we have not before now
been unacquainted with suffering), to these ills too god will grant an
end.'

How are the dynamics of incorporation here to be read? Despite the
systematic allusivity just mapped out, the tale of the further wanderings
of Diomedes at *Met.* 14.476–84 (a tiny miniature within the larger
miniature constituted by *Met.* 13.623–14.582) surely constitutes the
weakest of epigonal gestures towards the *Aeneid*, not a strong or dialogic
encounter with it. And yet, even as this Ovidian micro-tale assimilates
itself to the Virgilian master-text, its detailed points of resistance need to
be respected (e.g. the modest revision of Virgilian teleology lurking in
Met. 14.484[33]) – and even, perhaps, its own vestigial claims to set the
agenda.

On a closer inspection of the two death-wishes quoted above, one
intertextual detail stands out. Here again is the vocative address which
shapes the first speech of Virgil's Aeneas (1.96–7): *o Danaum fortissime
gentis / Tydide.* 'Son of Tydeus', Diomedes . . . On a 'normal' reading of
the *Aeneid*, an apostrophe spoken into the void. But now? Ovid's
Diomedeian repetition of the Virgilian death-wish reactivates that voca-
tive: on an Ovidian reading, Aeneas' *o . . . Tydide* becomes a 'cletic'
summons sent forward across intertextual time and space, which duly
elicits a 'response' from the Diomedes of the *Metamorphoses*, embarked
on his own mini-*Aeneid*. In this sense Aeneas' apostrophe is tendentious-
ly appropriated, even rewritten, by Ovid to become a kind of allusive
'cue' for Diomedes' own death-wish at *Met.* 14.480–2.[34] Against all the
odds, one of the most famous speeches in Virgil's *Aeneid* has become, for
just a moment, *pre-Ovidian*.

4 Unrepeatability

It is time for some general closing reflections. In the Diomedes of Ovid's
Aeneid, we find a vignette which, at the same time as it remakes a

---

[33] i.e. Ovid's repetition of the motif of the 'anticipated end of the comrades' sufferings'
ironically preempts the Virgilian *finem* (eventual colonization of Italy) with an
Ovidian one (immediate metamorphosis).

[34] And remember that the Iliadic encounter with Diomedes, in which the Virgilian
Aeneas would prefer to have died, is the very event which lies at the root of
Diomedes' own death-wish here in the *Metamorphoses* passage: cf. 14.477–8.

particular episode in Virgil's *Aeneid*, shows marked tendencies to double
the main Aeneas-narrative itself. In this latter sense it belongs with the
host of *non*-Virgilian tales earlier in the *Metamorphoses* which evoke and
engage with Virgilian types (cf. section 2 *init.*), such as the Theban cycle
and Phineus/Perseus, and with a host of east-to-west migrations with
post-Aeneian resonances in the final book of Ovid's epic.[35] Of all the
episodes in the *Metamorphoses* which have characters and situations
containing *any* kind of replay of the *Aeneid* a basic question can be asked
(corresponding to one of two which inaugurated section 1): how far is
the allusive analogy with the *Aeneid* to be pressed? An allusive relation-
ship, viewed in Contean terms as an analogical figure, is built upon a
perception of similarity and a perception of difference.[36] If difference
completely crowds out similarity, the figure vanishes – end of intertex-
tual story. If similarity completely crowds out difference, the intertextual
relationship moves from partial and figural iteration to *repetition pure
and simple* – so that episode after episode of the *Metamorphoses* turns
into the *Aeneid*.

   Since I have chosen in this chapter to focus on a case-study which
already shows some extremist tendencies, let me pursue this all the way
and ask hypothetically just what would happen if similarity *did* com-
pletely crowd out difference here in Ovid's *Aeneid*. Our poet's allusive
procedures in *Metamorphoses* 13.623–14.582 show how close he can
come to repeating the *Aeneid* in the *Metamorphoses* while still writing
poetry readable as Ovidian rather than as Virgilian. But let us suppose
(in a variant of Borges' Pierre Menard parable[37]) that Ovid's *Aeneid*,
instead of being a c.1,000–line *tour de force* of miniaturization, fore-
grounding, backgrounding and metapoetic commentary, were nothing

---

[35] Esp. Myscelus and Aesculapius; also Pythagoras and Hippolytus. The assimilation
of east-west migration stories to an Aeneian master-narrative is itself a Virgilian
move: cf. Barchiesi's 'Passages to Italy', cited in chapter 3, n.1.

[36] Conte (1986), 23–4 with 52–69.

[37] The hero of Borges' short story, 'Pierre Menard, Author of the *Quixote*', simulta-
neously embraces and problematizes the idea of '*total* identification with a given
author'. 'He did not want to compose another *Quixote* – which is easy – but *the
Quixote itself* . . . His admirable intention was to produce a few pages which would
coincide – word for word and line for line – with those of Miguel de Cervantes.'
Quotations from Borges (1964), 39; more (from 40) in my chapter epigraph. As
anticipated within the tale itself (44), it has become a favourite heuristic text for
students of the classical epic tradition.

less than a full and complete, word-for-word c.10,000–line *citation* of Virgil's *Aeneid* inside the closing books of the *Metamorphoses*. Common sense suggests that these 10,000 lines would now read as Virgil's rather than as Ovid's: but can we in fact be sure? Reframed by the Ovidian poetry of *Metamorphoses* 1–13 and *Metamorphoses* 14–15, the foreground and the background of the *Aeneid*-citation would not remain undisturbed. Even in the absence of the tendentious editing characteristic of Ovid's actual 1,000–line summary of the *Aeneid*, those hints of metamorphic narrative in Virgil's original 10,000–line *Aeneid* (the Trojan ships, Diomedes' companions etc.) would already feel different, would already send signals which they did not send before the *Aeneid* was *re-cited* in the middle of the *Metamorphoses*. The very teleology of the *Aeneid*, a profoundly Augustan teleology, would come under strong revisionary pressure from the rather different teleology of the framing *Metamorphoses*, and also (to historicize the point further) from the passage of real time – real history – in Augustan Rome between 19 BCE and 8 CE. What ironies, for instance, might the reader of 8–9 CE find in the verbatim re-citation of Virgil's *Aeneid* by a poet who has just himself been exiled by Aeneas' typological descendant from the homeland where Aeneas found deliverance from exile?[38] Repetition, it is clear, *always* entails some alteration.

However, an historicizing approach might tilt the master-text question (i.e. section 1's other inaugural question) back in an opposite direction too. Already at the time of the publication of the *Metamorphoses*, the *Aeneid* is such a culturally strong and authoritative text that any imitation runs the risk of being overwhelmed by it, of having its own textual integrity fragmented (another key term from early in the chapter) by the pressure of the *Aeneid*'s textuality. I have suggested that, when Ovid lets as much of the *Aeneid* into his poem as he does in *Metamorphoses* 13.623–14.582, he is able to resist the pressure and indeed to exert fragmenting pressures of his own on Virgil's epic. But if it really were all 10,000 lines of the *Aeneid* sitting inside the closing books of the *Metamorphoses* in a huge portmanteau-epic, what then? *Would* those 10,000 lines be attracted to an Ovidian agenda, as envisaged just above; or might it rather happen that the over-10,000 lines of *Metamorphoses* surrounding them would become somehow more Virgilian? Relative

---

[38] Cf. the ironies explored in an actual poem of 8–9 CE, Ovid's own *Trist.* 1.3.

cultural authority as between an incorporating and an incorporated text has much to do with how the balance of power between them will be constructed.[39]

And, in practice, this question of relative cultural authority can never be confined to the moment at which the incorporating text is produced: as exemplified in section 2, the relative authority of two texts will differ from one (subsequent) reader and reading community to another, as will *perceptions* of what the relative authority of the two texts was at that original moment of production. No two readings of the *Aeneid*, then, actual or hypothetical, poetic or literary critical, can ever be quite alike in their tendentiousness: even for Rome's most classic literary work, the price of poetic immortality (as Ovid might have accepted with more equanimity than Virgil) is endless unrepeatability.

[39] A point nowhere more emphatically felt than in ancient Homeric criticism: see e.g. Macrob. *Sat.* 6.3.1 on Homer as the rock which cannot be budged by intertextual buffeting.

5

Tradition and self-fashioning

When an allusion is organic rather than ornamental, when it is structurally necessary, then it begins to sketch a miniature myth about its own past, or rather about its emergence from that past. When in other words intertextuality becomes self-conscious, it tends to become etiological . . .

(Thomas Greene, *The Light in Troy*, 17–18)

Each new painting is a special case, acting in minute response to the innumerable images which compose its immediate neighbourhood. Each work will contain its own particular configuration of points of change, invocations and half-invocations, repetitions and deviations, a plurality of moments in which the tradition is locally called into being and then turned and troped.

(Norman Bryson, *Tradition and Desire*, 214)

1 Do-it-yourself literary tradition

My interest in allusive tendentiousness has taken me quite some way from a view of poetic tradition as an objective narrative focalized by an omniscient narrator. I should like in this final chapter to follow through on my own polemical emphasis, and to formulate as a counter-balance to the 'objectivist' model of literary history a '*subjectivist*' approach, which will use allusion to redescribe (the) tradition as, in effect, something mobilized by poets for the particular purposes of particular poems, and even for the particular purposes of particular moments in particular poems.

Both the first and last of my three case studies will take on the one-and-a-quarter book epic fragment which is the unfinished *Achilleid* of Statius – a poem (already glimpsed in chapter 3) just now emerging from the shadows into the bright light of the current Flavian revival. The very neglect of the *Achilleid* in modern times, the fact that fewer academic opinions have solidified around this epic than around any other in the classical Latin repertoire, perhaps gives rise to an opportunity: here, more (or differently) than in the case of the *Aeneid*, it may be possible to 'denature' the Roman epic tradition a little, and to (re)constitute it as something dynamic and open to appropriation.

I begin my exploration of the poem with an upside-down version of the approach which an objectivist literary historian might be expected to take. Rather than attempting to situate the *Achilleid* anew in literary history, I shall attempt to situate literary history anew in the *Achilleid*. That is to say, rather than taking as given a tradition, viz that of epic, which Statius inherits and against which his own *Achilleid* is to be measured, I want to read Statius not just as the creator of the *Achilleid* but also as the creator of traditions which he himself calls into being to account for the *Achilleid*-ness of the *Achilleid*. Statius' epic is to be read not in 'the' epic tradition but in *Statius'* epic tradition, which looks very much like the epic tradition familiar to us in narratives of literary history from Quintilian to Conte but is not – indeed cannot be – quite the same. This formulation may seem fussy, or like a statement of the obvious; but I hope to put it to good work before the end of the chapter.

Statius' citation of Homer's *Iliad* at the beginning of the *Achilleid*, already discussed in chapter 3, section 5, is as well known as anything in the interrupted epic, and is often cited as an instance of that deference to tradition which has been seen in modern scholarship, until very recently, as a debilitating feature of Statian poetry (1.3–5):

> . . . *quamquam acta viri multum inclita cantu*
> *Maeonio* (sed plura vacant), *nos ire per omnem –*
> sic amor est – *heroa velis* . . .

This is the literal extreme of what may be termed, à la chapter 1, a kind of literary historical self-annotation, whereby the poet intervenes as commentator on his own poetry's place in tradition.

Less direct is the element of literary historical self-annotation to be found in one of Statius' allusions to Catullus 64 – a poem always adduced as one of Statius' models in the *Achilleid*, but not normally in the way I have in mind.

It is no surprise that the *Peleus and Thetis* should be a model for Statius. That *tour de force* of epyllion, the closest and most sustained approximation to epic in Catullus' wary neoteric negotiations with the highest of genres, had already been effectively naturalized into full membership of the genre by the Augustans in their own allusive 'creations' of epic tradition (to make proleptic use of my tendentious vocabulary); and the subject of the completed portion of the *Achilleid*, the early youth of Achilles, offers a ready cue for allusion to Catullus' famous treatment of the wedding of his parents, in whose final quarter a prophetic song is sung by the *Parcae* concerning Achilles' own future life and death.

Two of Statius' clearest passages of allusion to Catullus 64, in fact, are targeted on the prophetic song of the *Parcae*. Early in *Achilleid* 1, when Neptune predicts to Thetis her son's notably bloody Trojan triumphs (1.84–9), the vignettes and many of the words draw on the song of the *Parcae* at Catullus 64.343–9 and 357–60. Later, in *Achilleid* 2, the hero himself recalls his boyhood training from Chiron (2.110–16),

> vix mihi bissenos annorum torserat orbes
> vita rudis, *volucres* cum iam *praevertere cervos*
> et Lapithas cogebat equos praemissaque *cursu*
> tela sequi; *saepe* ipse gradu me praepete Chiron,
> dum velox aetas, campis admissus agebat
> omnibus, exhaustumque *vago* per gramina *passu*
> laudabat gaudens . . .

Hardly had my raw youth turned the wheel of twice six years, when he drove me to outpace swift deer and Lapith horses, and to pursue at a race the dart flung ahead; often Chiron himself, while his age was yet nimble, chased me headlong at full gallop over all the plains, and when I was exhausted by ranging widely through the meadows he delighted to praise me

and again the language reconfigures one of the predictions of Catullus' *Parcae* concerning Achilles (64.340–1),

> qui persaepe vago victor certamine cursus
> flammea praevertet celeris vestigia cervae

Who full often victorious in the contest of the wide-ranging race will
outpace the fiery steps of the fleet she-deer . . .

That Statius' allusions are to Catullus 64 as a work of poetry, and not
just as a source for Achillean mythology, can be felt to emerge from the
emphatically placed allusion which takes up the last line of *Achilleid* 1.
Achilles leaves Deidamia, his love-interest, behind on Scyros; and the
book's closing vignette echoes Theseus' famous desertion of Ariadne on
the couch-coverlet in Catullus 64 – same poem as Peleus and Thetis, but
different myth, and different register of mimetic reality:

> *irrita ventosae* rapiebant verba *procellae*   (Statius, *Ach.* 1.960)

The inconstant gales swept his vain words away

> *irrita ventosae* linquens promissa *procellae*   (Catullus 64.59)

Leaving his vain promises to the inconstant gale . . .

Thus far the allusions are such as one would expect to find in a
conventional commentary; and one will indeed find them in Dilke's
useful but unadventurous 1954 commentary on the *Achilleid*.[1] However,
consider now an allusion to Catullus 64 earlier in *Achilleid* 1 which is not
described as such by Dilke. Thetis has come to Thessaly to see (and to
take away) her son, who is under the tutelage of Chiron; and, at the
centaur's instigation, the star pupil sings for his mother, accompanying
himself on the lyre (1.188–94):

> . . . *canit ille libens immania laudum*
> *semina*: quot tumidae superarit iussa novercae
> Amphitryoniades, crudum quo Bebryca caestu
> obruerit Pollux, quanto circumdata nexu
> ruperit Aegides Minoia bracchia tauri,
> *maternos in fine toros superisque gravatum*
> *Pelion* . . .

Gladly he sings of the mighty seeds of glorious deeds: how many tasks
set by his haughty stepmother Hercules accomplished, how Pollux

---

[1] Dilke (1954), 12 and ad locc.

with his glove smote down the cruel Bebryx, with what a grip Theseus enfolded and crushed the limbs of the Minoan bull, and lastly his own mother's conjugal couch and Pelion feeling the weighty presence of the gods . . .

It is a moment of intriguing literary self-referentiality. The climax of Achilles' song-sequence is nothing other than the wedding of Peleus and Thetis, which Statius thus designates as one of those heroic songs which deal with *immania laudum / semina* (in effect, κλέα ἀνδρῶν 'glorious deeds of men'; one recalls the Homeric vignette of Achilles singing in his tent in *Iliad* 9.189, itself by no means innocent of self-referential implication). Any doubt that Statius intends a metaliterary allusion to *Catullus'* song of Peleus and Thetis, in particular, should be dispelled by the sly metonymy in the phrase *maternos . . . toros*: already in Ovid's *Heroides* the 'couch' serves as a programmatic shorthand to specify allusion to Catullus 64, the marriage poem in which the couch itself quite literally dominates the action, through the famous ecphrastic description of its coverlet.[2] And if we press the metaliterary logic of the allusion a little, we may conclude that the *immania laudum / semina* celebrated by Achilles in this particular song are none other than his own – as recounted by the *Parcae* just before his conception (hence *laudum semina*?) in the last quarter of the 'original' Catullus 64.

Here, then, is the promised element of self-annotation. Not just an allusion to tradition, but allusion to the tradition *as* tradition. If the Iliadic reference in *Ach.* 1.3–5 is a literary historiographical citation, this is something less direct: perhaps we may call it a literary historiographical trope. Early in his opening book Statius has portrayed Achilles singing – maybe even composing – one of the source-texts for his own life, one of the source-texts for the present *Achilleid*; singing it, moreover, in juxtaposition with other songs which stake a claim (more straightforwardly than Catullus himself would have staked such a claim) for the wedding song of Peleus and Thetis to be classified as a heroic epic

---

[2] *Her.* 10.51–2 with Barchiesi (1993), 346–7, citing Verducci (1985), 262; also *Fast.* 3.484 *tam bene compositum . . . torum* 'such a harmonious couch'. Another specification of Catullus 64 is discernible in the immediately preceding Cretan vignette: 'the allusion to Catullus 64 begins with 191–2, so repeating what might seem to be the arbitrary juxtaposition of the Thetis and Ariadne stories in Catullus 64. [Statius'] *bracchia tauri* (192) unriddles the line-ending of Catullus 64.105' (Philip Hardie *per litteras*, with a brilliant flourish in the latter sentence).

narrative.[3] Troping the tradition *qua* tradition, the poet writes it into his poem.

Now this kind of metaliterary *jeu* has its own postmodern charm. What I want to emphasize here, however, is the way in which this, more deviously but no less significantly than the overt citation of the *Iliad* in the proem, marks an active intervention whereby the poet mobilizes the epic tradition for the particular purposes of his poem. Catullus 64 will be part of the epic matrix from which Statius' *Achilleid* will come anyway – how can it not be? – but Statius' literary historiographical troping of Catullus 64 changes the dynamic, positions Catullus 64 in a particular way within the tradition, ensures that *this* reading of the epic tradition, the epic tradition as seen from *and as written into* Statius' *Achilleid*, will not look quite like the epic tradition seen from any other vantage point.

It is worth setting this formulation in the context of a broader revisionist move in recent accounts of literary and artistic influence, which seeks to emphasize how the individual text or work acts upon its tradition as opposed to being acted upon by it. Such a move requires us, of course, to read against the grain of the words 'influence' and 'tradition' themselves. To end this first section, then, I invoke the elegant analogy in Michael Baxandall's *Excursus against influence*, in which (like his fellow art historian Norman Bryson, on whom more later) he is concerned to resist the classic formulation 'X influences Y', as in 'Cézanne influences Picasso':[4]

> The classic Humean image of causality that seems to colour many accounts of influence is one billiard ball, X, hitting another, Y. An image that might work better for the case would be not two billiard-balls but the field offered by a billiard table. On this table would be very many balls – the game is not billiards but snooker or pool – and the table is an Italian one without pockets. Above all, the cue-ball, that which hits another, is *not* X, but Y. What happens in the field,

---

[3] Not that anything but the need for argumentative brevity can justify use of the word 'straightforward' in connexion with any detail in this passage: e.g. on the heels of the vivid boxing and wrestling exploits of 190–2, and in consideration of the circumstances of Peleus' courtship of Thetis, can one avoid a fleeting but splendid misprision of *maternos... toros* in 193 as 'mother's *muscles*'? (A deviant reading, but one to which Hardie and I – again *per litteras* – found ourselves independently susceptible.) A robustly heroic Thetis, indeed!

[4] Baxandall (1985), 58–62 at 60.

each time Y refers to an X, is a rearrangement. Y has moved purpose-fully, impelled by the cue of intention, and X has been repositioned too: each ends up in a new relation to the array of all the other balls. Some of these have become more or less accessible or masked, more or less available to Y in his stance after reference to X. Arts are positional games and each time an artist is influenced he rewrites his art's history a little.

2 Local manipulation

Now for a different case, smaller-scale, within a slighter genre, but one which may serve to consolidate and advance the above line of inquiry. Section 1, seeking some room for manoeuvre within the strong narra-tives which constitute the epic tradition, has done little more than to highlight a *gesture* of literary historical self-annotation; section 2, away from the totalizing pressures of epic, will attempt a closer account of the dynamics of a particular allusion through which a poet writes literary tradition into one of his poems. A point not laboured above (or in chapter 1) will emerge more clearly here, namely that the self-annotation of *Ach.* 1.188–94 is not something exceptional, but rather an extreme manifestation of something always immanent in allusive discourse. My chosen example is also a collector's piece of intertextual ribaldry.

In the programmatic sequence of epigrams which opens his eleventh book, Martial welcomes and eulogizes the new government of Nerva; and he associates Nervan liberalization with the programme which he announces for his book, a programme which will indeed dominate it: a new accession of obscenity and uninhibited bawdiness (i.e. uninhibited even for Martial), for which the poet claims specifically Saturnalian licence (11.2.1–6):[5]

> triste supercilium durique severa Catonis
>   frons et aratoris filia Fabricia
> et personati fastus et regula morum
>   quidquid et in tenebris non sumus, ite foras.
> *clamant ecce mei 'Io Saturnalia' versus:*
>   et licet et sub te praeside, Nerva, libet

---

[5] Cf. Kay (1985), 5; the Saturnalian setting is further emphasized in 11.6.

Grim brow and stern countenance of rigid Cato and Fabricia, the
ploughman's daughter, and pride in its mask, and code of conduct,
and everything that in the dark we are not: out you go. Look, my
verses shout 'Ho for the Saturnalia!' Under your rule, Nerva, it is
both permitted and pleasing.

One poem in which Martial is as good as his word is 11.104, in which
the poet presents himself as castigating a woman, in very specific terms,
for her lack of sexual inventiveness in bed. What makes this epigram
especially striking and lascivious in terms of traditional decorum is that
the addressee is not the mistress of Augustan love elegy (more on the
appositeness of that standard of comparison in a moment), but the
poet's own wife.[6] Here is the opening couplet:

> uxor, vade foras aut moribus utere nostris:
> non sum ego nec Curius nec Numa nec Tatius

> Wife, get out or conform to my ways: I am no Curius or Numa or
> Tatius.

The first imperative probably parodies a Roman divorce formula[7] – and
it also wickedly doubles Martial's initial programmatic dismissal of stern
Cato-types from his poetry book: 11.104.1 *vade foras*, 11.2.4 *ite foras*.
    Let me focus attention on one of the poet-husband's many complaints
in this epigram, and on a particular mythological *exemplum* which
comes up within that complaint (11.104.11–16):

> nec motu dignaris opus nec voce iuvare
>   nec digitis, tamquam tura merumque pares:
> *masturbabantur Phrygii post ostia servi,*
>   *Hectoreo quotiens sederat uxor equo,*
> et quamvis Ithaco stertente pudica solebat
>   illic Penelope semper habere manum

> You don't deign to help the business along by movement or voice or
> fingers – as though you were preparing incense and wine. The
> Phrygian slaves used to masturbate behind the door as often as

---

[6] Or purported wife: Kay (1985) on 11.104 intro.   [7] Kay (1985) ad loc.

Hector's wife sat astride her 'horse', and even while Ulysses was snoring, modest Penelope always used to have her hand right there.

Lines 13–14 constitute a clear allusion to a couplet in the third book of Ovid's *Ars Amatoria*, in which the poet-teacher is making an argument that different sexual positions are appropriate to women of different builds (3.777–8):

> parva vehatur equo: *quod erat longissima, numquam*
> *Thebais Hectoreo nupta resedit equo*

A small woman should ride astride: because she was very tall, Hector's bride Andromache never sat astride her 'horse'.

Many things can be said about this allusion. A little facetiously, we can observe that Martial here shows himself adept at the principle of *oppositio in imitando*. Ovid offers one version of a tradition; Martial shows his independence of Ovid, and his own mythological learning, by contradicting this version of tradition: Andromache never rode astride Hector; well actually she did, all the time.

However, in my approach I want to go beneath the unimportant level at which Martial contradicts Ovid to a level at which he expresses a deeper continuity with Ovid; and I want to argue in the terms established in section 1 for the Statius-Catullus relationship. Thus I shall read Martial here not just as creator of the epigram *uxor, vade foras*, but also as creator of a tradition which he himself calls into being to account for the *uxor, vade foras*-ness of his *uxor, vade foras* epigram.

Here is my question: if we read Martial's couplet not in *the* tradition of the *Ars Amatoria* but in *Martial's* tradition of the *Ars Amatoria*, how does Martial's *Ars Amatoria* differ from the *Ars Amatoria* which we know and love? What, in other words, is tendentious about Martial's literary historical allusion?

Well, the seasoned reader of Ovid will recognize that the moment in the *Ars Amatoria* evoked here by Martial is far from typical of the poem. Contrary to its popular reputation, the *Ars Amatoria* is *not* an ancient precursor of *The Joy of Sex*. More than 95% of the poem is a manual of seduction and erotic intrigue – rich in innuendo to be sure, but in its approach to the mechanics of the sexual act as coy and indirect as is Augustan elegy at large. Only in the last 44 lines of Book 2, and in the last 44 lines of Book 3, does the logic of Ovid's start-to-finish approach to the conduct of a love intrigue bring his poem to the sexual act itself; and in each case Ovid self-consciously and programmatically acknowledges the crisis of decorum posed by this moment:

> *conscius, ecce, duos accepit lectus amantes:*
>   *ad thalami clausas, Musa, resiste fores.*
> sponte sua sine te celeberrima verba loquentur,
>   nec manus in lecto laeva iacebit iners;
> invenient digiti quod agant in partibus illis,
>   in quibus occulte spicula tingit Amor.
> fecit *in Andromache* prius hoc fortissimus *Hector*
>   nec solum bellis utilis ille fuit   (2.703–10)

Lo, the couch, privy to their union, has received two lovers: halt, Muse, at the closed doors of the bedroom. Of their own accord, without your aid, they will utter all those words, nor will the left hand lie idle in the bed; fingers will find what to do in those parts wherein Love secretly dips his darts. Most valiant Hector of old did thus with [or 'in'] Andromache, nor was his usefulness limited to war alone

> *ulteriora pudet docuisse, sed alma Dione*
>   *'praecipue nostrum est, quod pudet', inquit 'opus'.*
> nota sibi sit quaeque; modos a corpore certos
>   sumite: non omnes una figura decet . . .
> parva vehatur equo: *quod erat longissima, numquam*
>   *Thebais Hectoreo nupta resedit equo*   (3.769–72, 777–8)

What lies beyond I blush to teach; but kindly Dione says, 'What brings a blush is before all else my business'. Let each woman know herself; from your own bodies fix your methods: one position does not suit all alike . . . (etc.)

These more extended quotations from the *Ars* reveal that Ovid's graphic vignette of Hector and Andromache in bed, as visualized (and denied) in 3.777–8, belongs within the zone of greater sexual frankness introduced and problematized by Ovid at the end of *Ars* 3 as the women's book of seduction and intrigue nears its climax. Moreover, an earlier vignette of Hector and Andromache in bed is positioned in the equivalent zone at the end of the men's *Ars* late in Book 2. Indeed, Martial can be seen to have used *both* vignettes in 11.104.11–16: more obvious is the close verbal citation of the *Ars* 3 vignette; but the accompanying interest in vocal and digital encouragement derives, with a reversal of sex-roles, from the corresponding vignette at the end of *Ars* 2.

What I want to suggest, therefore, is that Martial is alluding, not to the *Ars Amatoria per se*, but to the sexually frank end-zones of the *Ars Amatoria*. Martial's *Ars Amatoria*, the *Ars* which Martial cites here in epigram 104, is not the one described in 'objectivist' literary histories, but a tendentious version of it. Martial writes into his epigram those specific sections of the *Ars* which already go half way towards meeting Martial's own sexually licentious poetic, and especially the intensification of licentiousness announced for his eleventh book. *This* reading of the *Ars*, the *Ars* called into being as tradition in the middle of this epigram of Martial, is an *Ars* with proto-Martialian tendencies, and will not look quite like the *Ars* read from any other vantage point.

What of the fact that 11.104.13–14 is just one couplet in one of over 100 epigrams in one of fifteen books by Martial? Even given some allowance for argumentative shorthand, is it not a little high-handed of me to use this one couplet in this one epigram to make grand claims about the literary historical relation of a Martialian to an Ovidian erotic aesthetic? Oddly enough, no – it is not. The subjectivist literary history formulated in this chapter differs from an objectivist literary history in being non-monolithic in tendency. Every allusion made by a poet, in epigram and epic alike, mobilizes its own *ad hoc* literary historical narrative – its own aetiology, as Thomas Greene would put it[8] – , and a subjectivized literary history is the total of many such narratives. (One might relate this perspective to broader theories of the subject which would hold that, in life itself as in literature, one's 'subjectivity' or 'identity' is not an unchanging essence, but rather a construct mobilized in different ways at different moments to meet different discursive needs.) I invoked above Michael Baxandall's account of how a work of art acts upon its tradition. A closer fit for the present case may be Norman Bryson's kindred formulation, quoted as the chapter's second epigraph, which (for us) differs most importantly from Baxandall's in its *atomization* of this narrative, in its emphasis upon 'acting in *minute* response', upon the '*particular* configuration of points of change', upon

---

[8] Greene (1982), 17–18, quoted as the chapter's first epigraph.

'a *plurality* of moments in which the tradition is locally called into being and then turned and troped'.[9]

Now although I want to signal the ability of such an interpretative strategy to privilege any and every moment in this way, my example at Martial 11.104.13–14 *is* an unusually marked one. Let us shift our attention within the couplet from the pentameter to the hexameter: we can no longer postpone discussion of those vigorous voyeurs behind the door of Hector and Andromache's bedroom, who add extra spice to Martial's version of the Ovidian mythological scene:

> masturbabantur Phrygii post ostia servi,
>   Hectoreo quotiens sederat uxor equo.

If the vignette in the pentameter is a clear allusion to the *Ars Amatoria*, what should we make of the slaves in the hexameter? Look again, not at the Hector–Andromache vignette in *Ars* 3, but at the Hector–Andromache vignette in *Ars* 2, from which we saw that Martial also draws some of his details. Immediately preceding the sex tips which Hector and Andromache proceed there to illustrate is Ovid's programmatic statement of his reticence about including such sex tips at all (2.703–4):

> conscius, ecce, duos accepit lectus amantes:
>   ad thalami clausas, Musa, resiste fores.

The Muse of Ovid's *Ars*, behind the bedroom door, is enjoined to hang coyly back from the action unfolding within; contrast Martial's slaves, *also* behind the door, who licentiously peep in and enjoy the action within in the most demonstrative and explicit way possible. Ovid's behind-the-door Muse embodies a principle of narrative coyness which is programmatic for the *Ars*'s whole approach to sex; and when they are recognized as transformations of that Muse, Martial's behind-the-door slaves can be seen to do the corresponding programmatic job for *his* whole book. The change from Muse to slave, the change from coy reticence to vigorous masturbation, tropes a 'lowering' of stylistic level – in Amy Richlin's suggestive term a 'staining' of the tradition[10] – firmly in

---

[9] Bryson (1984), 214 (emphs. mine). To juxtapose this with the Greene quotation is to invite some pressure upon the confident distinctions drawn in Greene's first two 'when' clauses.

[10] The term is introduced at Richlin (1992), 26–30. My treatment of Mart.

line with Martial's characteristic self-representation; and the fact that it is *slaves* who steal the Muse's role offers a specific dramatization of the poetics of Martial's eleventh book: the book of licentiousness, but also, specifically, the book of the Saturnalia, the festival at which normal social conventions and hierarchies are suspended or inverted, and in particular *slaves* are granted a temporary liberty to exceed the normal limits set on their conduct.[11]

To sum up this notable moment of self-fashioning: the Muse-like slaves' voyeurism in the face of the Ovidian bed-scene dramatizes and tropes Martial's own self-consciously voyeuristic and Saturnalian appropriation of his predecessor's erotic aesthetic. Seldom has literary history been so graphically handled.

3 In search of Achilles

After that carnivalesque stopover with Hector, my final case study returns to the world of Statius' *Achilleid*. In Book 1 of the *Achilleid*, Statius portrays Thetis' coaxing introduction of Achilles to Scyros, where he is to live as a simulant woman among women (1.319–20, 335–7):

> '*hasne inter simulare choros* et bracchia ludo
> nectere, nate, grave est? . . . '
>   . . . superest nam plurimus illi
> invita virtute decor, *fallit*que tuentes
> *ambiguus* tenuique latens *discrimine* sexus

'Is it so hard a thing, my son, to pretend a role within this female band and to join hands with them in sport?' . . . For an abundance of gracefulness is at Achilles' disposal, his manly vigour notwithstanding, and beholders are misled by an indeterminate sex that by a narrow distinction hides its secret.

Horace, at the end of his Lalage Ode, implicitly compares to Achilles on Scyros a certain androgynous youth named Gyges (*Carm.* 2.5.21–4),[12]

11.104.13–14 may perhaps be read, then, as an elaboration along Richlinian lines of Richlin (1992), 158–60.

[11] Cf. Kay (1985) on Mart. 11.6, intro. with references.

[12] On the implicit evocation of Achilles on Scyros at Horace, *Carm.* 2.5.21–4 cf. Nisbet

> *quem si puellarum insereres choro,*
> mire sagaces *falleret* hospites
> *discrimen* obscurum solutis
> crinibus *ambiguo*que vultu

[Gyges] whom if you set amid a band of girls, discerning guests would be wondrously misled by the obscuring of distinction in his flowing tresses and indeterminate face.

Statius has 'recognized' and appropriated a veiled reference to Achillean myth in Horace: this is one of the clearest verbal and situational allusions to be found anywhere in the *Achilleid*.[13] Let me ask a question about it, and propose a rather unexpected answer.

Question: Is Statius alluding here to Horace's *Odes*? Answer: No, he is alluding to Ovid's *Metamorphoses*.

Why such an answer, which perversely ignores the evidence set out above, italicized correspondences and all? What I am proposing is a paradoxical half-truth rather than the whole truth – but it is a paradoxical half-truth worth investigating.

The combination of being a fragment and being by Statius has proved near-fatal to the *Achilleid* in modern times. Those few critics who have paused to consider the poem have been struck above all by dominant qualities of playfulness and whimsy unexpected in an epic by the author of the *Thebaid*, or indeed in any epic.[14] It is significant that genre-labels *other* than 'epic' have tended to be used to describe the *Achilleid*. It has been described as 'bucolic'; its affinities with new comedy have been stressed; to Conte it is 'relaxed and *idyllic*'; to Feeney a 'charming, almost *novelistic*, fragment'.[15] However, in the past two or three years a handful of readers (all, as it happens, authors of published or planned books on Ovid's *Metamorphoses*) have independently returned to an epic paradigm in their characterizations of the poem: it *is* an epic: a

and Hubbard (1978) ad loc.

[13] Cf. Dilke (1954) on 1.336–7 ' . . . three important words are reproduced'; Rosati (1994b), 14–15.

[14] . . . whether these qualities were destined to obtain throughout the *Achilleid*, or whether (as is often assumed) it is just that the early days of Achilles determine the character of the completed book and a quarter. Cf. n.26 below.

[15] For these labels (emphs. mine) see respectively Jannaccone (1947–50), 79; Koster (1979), 206–8 and other discussions cited in Rosati (1994a), 57n.35 = (1994b), 25n.38; Conte (1994b), 487; Feeney (1991), 376n.199.

markedly *Ovidian*, markedly *metamorphic* epic.[16] Young love in an un-
warlike land secluded from the outside world; an uneasy mixture of
courtship and rape; disguise, deception, cross-dressing, ambiguities of
sex, gender and identity: this is not the core stuff of Roman epic at large
(except in its interludes); but it *is* the core subject-matter of Ovid's
particular brand of epic. (I shall approach the Ovidianism itself now,
and return to its generic implications later.)

I want to focus on the last and most striking elements in my catalogue:
disguise, deception, cross-dressing, ambiguities of sex, gender and ident-
ity. These are central to the narrative treatment of Achilles on Scyros in
Achilleid 1; and the air which that narrative breathes is very much the air
of Ovid's *Metamorphoses*. (My reading here overlaps with and draws on
that of Gianpiero Rosati in his already foundational 1994 work on the
Achilleid.[17]) Consider the behavioural details in Achilles' reluctance to
don women's clothes, and Thetis' assurance that his rugged tutor Chiron
need never know (1.270–4); the titillating description of the first stages of
Achilles' courtship of Deidamia, featuring Deidamia's initially unsus-
pecting but growingly complicit acquiescence in the more-than-girl-
friend-like intensity and physicality of Achilles' attentions (1.564–91); or
the tension at the royal banquet, later in the book, between an Achilles
buckling under the strain of playing the girl, a Deidamia covering up for
him, and a Ulysses who is missing absolutely nothing (1.761–811). Such
vignettes might all be described in general terms as 'Hellenistic'.[18] But on
my instinct at least (as on Rosati's), it is hard to imagine Statius playing
these scenes in quite this way, with quite this tone, without the precedent
of Ovid's *Metamorphoses*. Indeed – to make explicit the claim which has
been building over the past page, viz that the new wave of reception of
the *Achilleid* as an Ovidian poem is in sympathy with Statius' own
allusive aetiology – it can be argued that the preface to the courtship
episode in effect 'cites' the *Metamorphoses* as inspiration by describing

---

[16] I thus align myself with Gianpiero Rosati in (1994a and b), as also with Philip
Hardie in (1993), 63n.8 (quoted in n.26). For anticipations cf. Koster (1979);
Fantham (1979), 457.

[17] Rosati (1994a), 53–9, and (1994b), 25–33.

[18] Current work on the *Achilleid* by Alessandro Barchiesi – another Ovidian –
promises to particularize 'Hellenistic' as in some instances 'Apollonian'. The frag-
mentary idyll on Achilles and Deidamia formerly attributed to Bion bears direct
witness to the appeal of Achilles on Scyros to a Hellenistic poetic sensibility.

Achilles' assumed form in a phrase familiar from Ovid's epic as a formula for metamorphic change:

> at procul occultum *falsi sub imagine* sexus
> Aeaciden furto iam noverat una latenti
> Deidamia virum . . .   (1.560–2)

But, far off, Deidamia alone in stolen secrecy had come to know Achilles, though hidden under the form of a feigned sex, as a man

> dilacerant *falsi* dominum *sub imagine* cervi   (Ovid, *Met.* 3.250)

> . . . nati furta, iuvencum,
> occuluit Liber *falsi sub imagine* cervi . . .   (Ovid, *Met.* 7.359–60)[19]

Material like this, and much more besides, adds up to a sustained vein of allusion in the *Achilleid* to a distinctively Ovidian narrative aesthetic. In many passages the engagement consists less in specific verbal allusions than in an ambience, a narrative decorum, a distinctive way of envisaging and deploying an intrigue of sex, gender and identity. It might be said that, in some phases of this relationship, specific verbal allusions, where they exist, do not so much *constitute* the intertextual debt, which would be there without them, as *footnote* it.

It is time to revisit the passage with which this section began, the passage in which Thetis coaxes Achilles into his female disguise. In my earlier quotation I skipped with an ellipsis from the beginning of the scene to its end. Here is some of the intervening action (1.326–8, 332–4):

> . . . tum colla rigentia mollit
> submittitque graves umeros et fortia laxat
> bracchia . . .
> qualiter artifici victurae pollice cerae
> accipiunt formas ignemque manumque sequuntur,
> *talis erat divae natum mutantis imago*

Then she softens his stiff neck and bows his heavy shoulders and relaxes his strong arms . . . Even as waxen images, that the artist's thumb will bring alive, take on form, following the fire and the hand: such was the picture of the goddess as she transformed her son.

---

[19] Tr.: 'they mangle their master *under the form of the feigned* stag'; 'Liber hid his son's theft, the steer, *under the form of a feigned* stag'.

What is this but an Ovidian metamorphosis, with Thetis as the divine agent? In the wax-modelling simile (*qualiter artifici <u>victurae</u> pollice cerae*) there may even be a specific allusion to Pygmalion, whose metamorphic way with art in Ovid's tenth book invites programmatic comparison with the *Metamorphoses'* own artistic project.[20] Be that as it may, the account of Thetis in action certainly sustains our broad pattern of a symptomatically Ovidian narrative aesthetic. And symptomatic too, as we reapproach the crux of the matter, are numerous parallels in Ovid's *Metamorphoses* for the puzzling androgyny which is now attributed to the cross-dressed Achilles as Thetis ends her exertions – in the lines already quoted at the outset of this section (*Ach.* 1.335–7):

> nec luctata diu; superest nam plurimus illi
> invita virtute decor, fallitque tuentes
> ambiguus tenuique latens discrimine sexus

Compare, in the *Metamorphoses*, the ambiguous gender of Sithon (4.279–80),

> . . . ut quondam naturae iure novato
> ambiguus fuerit modo vir, modo femina Sithon

of Salmacis/Hermaphroditus (4.378–9),

> . . . nec femina dici
> nec puer ut possit, neutrumque et utrumque videntur

of Atalanta (8.322–3),

> talis erat cultu, facies, quam dicere vere
> virgineam in puero, puerilem in virgine possis

of Iphis (9.712–13),

> cultus erat pueri; facies, quam sive puellae
> sive dares puero, fuerat formosus uterque

---

[20] On Pygmalion and Ovid as metamorphic artists, cf. Rosati (1983); Solodow (1988), 215–19. Pygmalion's statue is made of ivory, but at the moment of transformation (*Met.* 10.282–6) its texture is likened to wax softening and being moulded by the thumb.

or, indeed, of Bacchus (4.18–20).[21] Compare also, perhaps, the eye-deceiving aesthetic of the virtuoso tapestry-work which emblematizes Ovid's art at *Met.* 6.61–6:

> illic et Tyrium quae purpura sensit aenum
> texitur et tenues parvi discriminis umbrae;
> qualis ab imbre solet percussis solibus arcus
> inficere ingenti longum curvamine caelum;
> in quo diversi niteant cum mille colores,
> transitus ipse tamen spectantia lumina fallit

Woven in are purple threads dyed in Tyrian vats, and delicate shades with fine distinctions; as when the sun's rays are struck by a shower, and a rainbow with its huge curve tints the wide sky; and a thousand different colours shine in it, yet the change from each to the next misleads the watching eye . . .

Symptomatic parallels. Nevertheless (to return to the paradox of my inaugural question and answer) it remains no less clear on the basis of the strongest possible verbal and situational correspondences that the specific target of the allusion in *Ach.* 1.335–7 is none of these metamorphic passages, but rather Horace, *Carm.* 2.5.21–4, the implicitly mythological vignette at the end of the Lalage Ode. But it should now be emerging why I answered my question as I did.

I submit that there *is* a point of view from which Horace's Lalage Ode is here not to serve a Horatian agenda, but to contribute to a broader pattern in the *Achilleid* which is unmistakeably an Ovidian one. One way to make this case (cf. chapter 4, section 1) would be to say that a 'local' approach to allusion, an approach which privileges the individual highly wrought moment, will read Horace, *Carm.* 2.5 here, *qua* Horace, *Carm.* 2.5, as a privileged source; but that a 'systematic' approach may well read the allusion to Horace, *Carm.* 2.5 as an epiphenomenal piece of Horatian local colour in a broad pattern of narrative allusion which is firmly constituted as Ovidian.

---

[21] Trs: 'how once Sithon, the natural laws changed, lived of indeterminate sex, now man and now woman'; 'so that they can neither be styled woman nor boy: they seem to be neither and both'; 'such was her dress, and her face such as you might truly say was maidenly for a boy or boyish for a maiden'; 'the dress was a boy's; the face such that, whether you gave it to a girl or a boy, either would have been counted beautiful'.

I believe that the local/systematic distinction is a helpful one in this case. However, as literary historical subjectivists, we should not omit to acknowledge that 'local' and 'systematic' are themselves negotiable categories, which cannot always be relied upon to remain wholly stable and objective. In Horace's *Odes* the androgynous Achilles is a figure met on another occasion too, this time explicitly, at *Carm.* 1.8.13–16, a figure not without some potential to suggest or symbolize Horace's larger appropriation into lyric of the motives of martial epic myth. To deny to Statius' Horatian allusion at *Ach.* 1.335–7 the possibility of opening out into a systematic pattern of its own (even, ultimately, into an aetiological reading of the *Achilleid* as in some sense a 'Horatian' epic) might be hasty.[22] Let us be alert, then, to two differently tendentious narratives which can be mobilized at this point in the text of the *Achilleid*, one Horatiocentric and one Ovidiocentric; but, having allowed that much, let us continue to explore the claim of the Ovidiocentric narrative to be the dominant one.

In the one-to-one allusive correspondence initially revealed by my reading in isolation of *Ach.* 1.335–7, the dynamics of appropriation were ready to be acted out between two terms, one Statian and one Horatian. However, a broader framing of the allusive event in these more recent pages has added a third term. To repeat the question asked of other allusive events in this chapter: if we read Statius' allusion to Horace, *Carm.* 2.5 not in *the* tradition of Horace, *Carm.* 2.5 but in *Statius'* tradition of Horace, *Carm.* 2.5, how does Statius' Horace differ from the Horace whom we know from elsewhere? One possible answer can say: *not* he is more *Statian*; but rather, he is more *Ovidian*. More precisely, Statius has appropriated Horace not just to a Statian poem, but to a Statian poem's appropriation of an Ovidian poem.

Now there is available a good classical word, much used (or misused) by modern Latin philologists, to smooth over this paradox: *contaminatio*.[23] What I have been doing, in effect, is considering a common inter-

---

[22] For suggestive remarks on Achilles and Horace's lyric poetics see Leach (1994); further discussion can be anticipated in Michèle Lowrie's forthcoming book on narrative in the *Odes*. Note with Rosati (1994b), 15n.22, the after-echo of Horace, *Carm.* 2.5.22 at *Ach.* 1.817–18 *sagaci . . . Ithaco* 'the discerning Ithacan'.

[23] See e.g. (including discussion of the modern philological usage as a misrepresentation of ancient usage) West and Woodman (1979), index s.v.

textual situation from an uncommon angle.[24] Faced with a text which engages simultaneously with two prior texts, orthodox allusive criticism speaks of the alluding author as 'contaminating' the two model texts. What tends to be deadened in such a description is, precisely, the *dynamic* involved in any such appropriation. How is the balance of power to be configured in such a meeting of texts? Which text, and whose appropriative emphasis in which text, is foregrounded? And even if these terms can be held still, what about the moment-to-moment shifts in emphasis and balance which are part of any one writer's or reader's experience of getting a purchase on any intertextual nexus?

4   Genre, history, subjectivity

Let me draw out two concluding but also open-ended thoughts. If Statius' account of Achilles on Scyros systematically alludes to an Ovidian narrative decorum, as I have suggested in section 3, why is the standard commentary on the *Achilleid* silent about the Ovidian connexions of virtually every passage I have discussed?[25] Why, until the intervention of a clutch of *fin de siècle* Ovidian commentators in the 1990s, have the dominant adjectives applied to the *Achilleid* in modern times been 'bucolic', 'idyllic', 'new comic' and 'novelistic', rather than 'Ovidian', 'metamorphic' and 'epic'? Not, I think, because the Ovidiocentrists have tendentiously inflated the importance to Statius of these Ovidian connexions (though such a case can no doubt be made).

Rather because – and here we come up against one of the limits of allusive self-fashioning – this aspect of Statius' own bid to write the tradition into his poem has been, measured by its modern reception, a failure. Statius' literary historiography in the unfinished *Achilleid* constructs an epic tradition in which Ovid's *Metamorphoses* features front and centre.[26] This is a tendentious reading of literary history by Statius

---

[24] I feel some tactical affinity here with Thomas's (1986), 190–3, use of paradox to set up his category of 'apparent reference'.

[25] i.e. Dilke (1954). One exception: an Ovidian 'cf.' at *Ach.* 1.560 *falsi sub imagine*.

[26] At least, that is, in its completed portion. For the likely continuation in some form of an Ovidian agenda cf. the poem's programmatic preface at *Ach.* 1.4–7 (quoted chapter 3, section 5), with the (compressed) gloss of Hardie (1993), 63n.8: 'by his use of the Ovidian *deducere* (*Met.* 1.4) at *Ach.* 1.7 "to lead the youth through the whole story of Troy" *tota iuvenem deducere Troia*, Statius signals that this epic will be an Ovidian "continuous song" *perpetuum carmen*'; cf. Koster (1979), 195–6.

– more obviously tendentious than his privileging of Catullus 64 – and evidently it is one which has not become canonical. The fact that most modern critics have found the poem unepic, the fact that, while noting individual *loci similes* or traits of style, they have not felt the poem to be in any sense *systematically* Ovidian, shows that (in Contean terms) the *Metamorphoses* has not been arriving to most readers as a 'code model' for the *Achilleid*.[27] And the truth is that the Roman epic code at large never in this sense fully assimilated the *Metamorphoses*; it remained an anomaly within the genre. It was Virgil, not Ovid, who provided the code model for the most influential epic poems written in the hundred years or so after his death – including Statius' own earlier epic, the *Thebaid*. Ovid himself had of course already problematized the epic status of his *Metamorphoses*; and if readers nineteen hundred years after the composition of the *Achilleid* fail to pick up a strand of literary historical aetiology which characterizes the *Achilleid* as a post-Metamorphic epic, that is less a matter of simple inattention than it is a matter of Statius having here shifted the epic paradigm in a direction which was resistant to the previous (and perhaps to the subsequent) history of the genre. Working against Statius' tendentious literary historiography was not only the extraordinarily durable Roman theorization of the default setting of epic as *res gestae regumque ducumque et tristia bella* 'achievements of kings and generals and grim wars' (Horace, *A.P.* 73), but also the cumulative Virgiliocentric history of epic construction and reception which had already in Flavian times taken firm hold, and had declined to coopt the bold Ovidian experiment to the mainstream of the genre. In other words, if the history of Roman epic had developed in a more Ovidiocentric way, more twentieth-century readers might see more Ovid in the *Achilleid* than they do.[28]

The literary historiographical control exercised by the alluding poet can be destabilized, in other words, by the circumstances of reception, by the fact that his literary history is in competition with the literary histories constructed by countless other poets and readers throughout

---

[27] 'Modello-codice': Conte (1986), 31; cf. chapter 2, section 4 above.

[28] Pertinent here are the comments of Martindale (1993), 59, on how the *Metamorphoses*, 'generically skewed as an epic', became orthodox and normative only when it was 're-emplotted' as a *romance* by Renaissance theorists.

time – a point already adumbrated at the end of chapter 4.[29] My other approach to the limits of allusive self-fashioning offers a more radical destabilization still. The fact is that the alluding poet is in competition as a literary historian not just with his predecessors, successors and readers: he is also in competition with himself. Again, this can be sufficiently dramatized by the allusion just investigated, in which, as I have shown, a clear Statius/Horace dynamic can be contested in the *Achilleid*'s own terms (even down to moment-to-moment shifts in emphasis and balance) by a Statius/Ovid dynamic – and *vice versa*. The creative imagination is an endlessly mobile thing; and not even through the most apparently objectively verifiable allusion (such as Statius' here to Horace, *Carm.* 2.5.21–4) can access ultimately be gained to what an alluding poet at any given moment *intended* by such an allusion.

However, it would be a mistake (a common mistake, to be sure) to take this as a reason to lose our curiosity about what poets mean to do when they allude. (I return in this final paragraph to an affirmation made in chapter 2, section 5.) It is inevitable that a subjectivist approach to literary tradition, by assigning such an important role to the self-fashioning poet, should run up against that famous (and undeniable) *impasse*, the ultimate unknowability of the poet's intention. We cannot afford to treat this as an invitation to unconditional surrender. The fact is that in authorial subjectivity we have one of our best and most enabling terms to conceptualize the partiality, and interestedness, of any construction of literary tradition, any version of literary history – our own included. Let us grant (as grant we must) that the self-fashioning, intention-bearing poet is a figure whom we ourselves read out from the text to test our readings in an interpretative move which is necessarily circular: yet the energy generated by this interpretative circulation is very real. Without some idea of the poet as aetiologist, as mobilizer of his own tradition, ever tendentious and ever manipulative, *our* accounts of literary tradition will always turn out too flat. If we are to dramatize the immediacy of the interests at stake in the dynamics of appropriation, we must be prepared to personalize them.

---

[29] It may be no accident of timing that my own narrative of the skewing of Statius' *Achilleid* as an epic should find its point of access, like so many late twentieth-century readings of classic texts, in a nexus which destabilizes norms of *gender* as well as of *genre*. (Exchanges with Tom Habinek and Alison Keith prompt such historicization of my own reading.)

Bibliography

Aicher, P. (1989) 'Roman poetry and the anxiety of influence', *American Philological Association 120th Annual Meeting: Abstracts.* Atlanta

Anderson, W. S. (1982) 'Part versus whole in Persius' fifth satire', in *Essays on Roman Satire.* Princeton, 153–68

Badian, E. (1972) 'Ennius and his friends', in *Ennius*, Entretiens Hardt 17. Geneva, 149–208

Baldo, G. (1986) 'Il codice epico nelle Metamorfosi di Ovidio', *MD* 16: 109–31

Barchiesi, A. (1984) *La traccia del modello: Effetti omerici nella narrazione virgiliana.* Pisa

(1986) 'Problemi d'interpretazione in Ovidio: continuità delle storie, continuazione dei testi', *MD* 16: 77–107

(1993) 'Future reflexive: two modes of allusion and Ovid's *Heroides*', *HSCP* 95: 333–65

Barchiesi, M. (1962) *Nevio epico.* Padua

Barkan, L. (1991) *Transuming Passion: Ganymede and the Erotics of Humanism.* Stanford

Barthes, R. (1979) *A Lover's Discourse: Fragments*, trans. R. Howard. London

(1989) 'The death of the author', in *The Rustle of Language*, trans. R. Howard. Berkeley, 49–55

Baxandall, M. (1985) *Patterns of Intention: On the Historical Explanation of Pictures.* New Haven

Ben-Porat, Z. (1976) 'The poetics of literary allusion', *PTL* 1: 105–28

Bing, P. (1988) *The Well-Read Muse: Present and Past in Callimachus and the Hellenistic Poets.* Göttingen

Borges, J. L. (1964) 'Pierre Menard, author of the *Quixote*', in *Labyrinths.* New York, 36–44

Bourdieu, P. (1984) *Distinction: A Social Critique of the Judgement of Taste*, trans. R. Nice. Cambridge

Bowie, A. M. (1990) 'The death of Priam: allegory and history in the *Aeneid*', *CQ* 40: 470–81

Bramble, J. C. (1974) *Persius and the Programmatic Satire.* Cambridge

Brink, C. O. (1963–82) *Horace on Poetry.* 3 vols. Cambridge

Bryson, N. (1984) *Tradition and Desire: From David to Delacroix.* Cambridge

Clausen, W. V. (1964) 'Callimachus and Latin poetry', *GRBS* 5: 181–96

(1994) *A Commentary on Virgil, Eclogues.* Oxford

Coleman, K. M. (1988) *Statius: Silvae IV.* Oxford

Connors, C. (1998) *Petronius the Poet: Verse and Literary Tradition in the Satyricon.* Cambridge

Conte, G. B. (1981) 'A proposito dei modelli in letteratura', *MD* 6: 147–60

(1984) *Virgilio: Il genere e i suoi confini.* Milan

(1985) *Memoria dei poeti e sistema letterario*, rev. ed. Turin

(1986) *The Rhetoric of Imitation: Genre and Poetic Memory in Virgil and Other Latin Poets*, ed. C. Segal. Ithaca

(1994a) *Genres and Readers*, trans. G. W. Most. Baltimore

(1994b) *Latin Literature: A History*, trans. J. B. Solodow. Baltimore

Conte, G. B. and Barchiesi, A. (1989) 'Imitazione e arte allusiva. Modi e funzioni dell' intertestualità', in *Lo spazio letterario di Roma antica*, I. Rome, 81–114

Courtney, E. (1993) *The Fragmentary Latin Poets.* Oxford

Crowther, N. B. (1971) 'Catullus and the traditions of Latin poetry', *CP* 66: 246–8

(1976) 'Parthenius and Roman poetry', *Mnemosyne* 29: 65–71

(1980) 'Parthenius, Laevius and Cicero: hexameter poetry and Euphorionic myth', *LCM* 5: 181–3

Curtius, E. R. (1953) *European Literature and the Latin Middle Ages*, trans. W. R. Trask. London

Davies, P. V. (1969) *Macrobius: The Saturnalia.* New York

Dewar, M. (1994) 'Laying it on with a trowel: the proem to Lucan and related texts', *CQ* 44: 199–211

Dilke, O. A. W. (1954) *Statius: Achilleid.* Cambridge

Eco, U. (1990) *The Limits of Interpretation.* Bloomington

(1992) *Interpretation and Overinterpretation*, ed. S. Collini. Cambridge

Edwards, C. (1993) *The Politics of Immorality in Ancient Rome.* Cambridge

Ernout, A. and Meillet, A. (1959) *Dictionnaire étymologique de la langue latine.* 4th ed. Paris

Esposito, P. (1994) *La narrazione inverosimile: Aspetti dell' epica ovidiana.* Naples

Fantham, E. (1979) 'Statius' Achilles and his Trojan model', *CQ* 29: 457–62

(1982) *Seneca's Troades.* Princeton

(1990) '*Nymphas . . . e navibus esse*: decorum and poetic fiction in *Aeneid* 9.77–122 and 10.215–59', *CP* 85: 102–19

(1992) *Lucan: De Bello Civili Book II.* Cambridge

Farrell, J. (1991) *Vergil's Georgics and the Traditions of Ancient Epic.* Oxford

Feeney, D. C. (1986) 'History and revelation in Vergil's underworld', *PCPS* 32: 1–24

(1991) *The Gods in Epic: Poets and Critics of the Classical Tradition.* Oxford

(1992) '"Shall I compare thee . . . ?": Catullus 68b and the limits of analogy', in A. J. Woodman and J. Powell (eds.), *Author and Audience in Latin Literature.* Cambridge, 33–44

(1998) *Literature and Religion at Rome: Cultures, Contexts, and Beliefs.* Cambridge

Felperin, H. (1990) *The Uses of the Canon: Elizabethan Literature and Contemporary Theory.* Oxford

Fowler, D. P. (1989) 'First thoughts on closure: problems and prospects', *MD* 22: 75–122

(1991) Subject review of Roman literature, *G&R* 38: 85–97

Galinsky, G. K. (1975) *Ovid's Metamorphoses: An Introduction to the Basic Aspects.* Oxford

Genette, G. (1982) *Palimpsestes: la littérature au second degré.* Paris

Goldberg, S. M. (1995) *Epic in Republican Rome.* Oxford

Goldhill, S. (1991) *The Poet's Voice: Essays on Poetics and Greek Literature.* Cambridge

Gordon, R. L. (1979) 'The real and the imaginary: production and religion in the Graeco-Roman world', *Art History* 2: 5–34

Gowing, A. M. (1997) 'Greek advice for a Roman senator: Cassius Dio and the dialogue between Philiscus and Cicero (38.18–29)', *PLLS* forthcoming

Greene, T. M. (1982) *The Light in Troy: Imitation and Discovery in Renaissance Poetry.* New Haven

Gruen, E. S. (1990) *Studies in Greek Culture and Roman Policy.* Leiden

Häussler, R. (1976) *Das historische Epos der Griechen und Römer bis Vergil.* Heidelberg

Hardie, P. (1990) 'Ovid's Theban history: the first "Anti-*Aeneid*"?', *CQ* 40: 224–35

(1992) 'Augustan poets and the mutability of Rome', in A. Powell (ed.), *Roman Poetry and Propaganda in the Age of Augustus.* London, 59–82

(1993) *The Epic Successors of Virgil: A Study in the Dynamics of a Tradition.* Cambridge

Hartman, G. H. (1983) 'Reading aright: Keats's *Ode to Psyche*', in E. Cook et al. (eds.), *Centre and Labyrinth.* Toronto, 210–26

Henderson, J. G. W. (1987) 'Lucan/the word at war', *Ramus* 16: 122–64

(1993) 'Form remade/Statius' *Thebaid*', in A. J. Boyle (ed.), *Roman Epic.* London, 162–91

Hinds, S. E. (1985) 'Booking the return trip: Ovid and *Tristia* 1', *PCPS* 31: 13–32

(1987a) *The Metamorphosis of Persephone: Ovid and the Self-Conscious Muse.* Cambridge

(1987b) 'Generalising about Ovid', *Ramus* 16: 4–31

(1992) '*Arma* in Ovid's *Fasti*', *Arethusa* 25: 81–153

(1993) 'Medea in Ovid: scenes from the life of an intertextual heroine', *MD* 30: 9–47

Hollander, J. (1981) *The Figure of Echo: A Mode of Allusion in Milton and After.* Berkeley

Hollis, A. S. (1977) *Ovid: Ars Amatoria Book 1.* Oxford

Horsfall, N. (1990) 'Virgil and the illusory footnote', *PLLS* 6: 49–63

Jannaccone, S. (1947–50) 'Quo artificio P. Papinius Statius Achilleidi condendae operam dederit', *Antiquitas* 2–5: 79–83

Jocelyn, H. D. (1972) 'The poems of Quintus Ennius', *ANRW* I. 2, 987–1026

Johnson, W. R. (1987) *Momentary Monsters: Lucan and his Heroes.* Ithaca

Kaster, R. A. (1978) 'Servius and *idonei auctores*', *AJP* 99: 181–209

(1992) *Studies on the Text of Suetonius De Grammaticis et Rhetoribus*. Atlanta

Kay, N. M. (1985) *Martial Book XI*. London

Kearns, J. M. (1990) 'ΣΕΜΝΟΤΗΣ and dialect gloss in the *Odussia* of Livius Andronicus', *AJP* 111: 40–52

Keith, A. M. (1991) 'Etymological play on *ingens* in Ovid, Vergil, and *Octavia*', *AJP* 112: 73–6

(1992) '*Amores* 1.1: Propertius and the Ovidian programme', *Collection Latomus* 217: 327–44

Kennedy, D. F. (1993) *The Arts of Love: Five Studies in the Discourse of Roman Love Elegy*. Cambridge

(1995) Subject review of Roman literature, *G&R* 42: 83–8

Kermode, F. (1983) *Essays on Fiction 1971–82*. London

Knapp, S. and Michaels, W. B. (1982) 'Against theory', *Critical Inquiry* 8: 723–42

Koster, S. (1979) 'Liebe und Krieg in der "Achilleis" des Statius', *Würzb. Jahrbb. Altertumsw.* n.F.5: 189–208

Krevans, N. (1993) 'Fighting against Antimachus: the *Lyde* and the *Aetia* reconsidered', in M. A. Harder et al. (eds.), *Callimachus*. Groningen, 149–60

Kroll, W. (1924) *Studien zum Verständnis der römischen Literatur*. Stuttgart

Labate, M. (1990) 'Forme della letteratura, immagini del mondo: da Catullo a Ovidio', *Storia di Roma*, 2.1. Turin, 923–65

Leach, E. W. (1994) 'Horace *Carmen* 1.8: Achilles, the Campus Martius, and the articulation of gender roles in Augustan Rome', *CP* 89: 334–43

Lee, A. G. (1971) 'Allusion, parody and imitation'. St. John's College Cambridge Lecture. Hull

Lyne, R. O. A. M. (1978) 'The neoteric poets', *CQ* 28: 167–87

(1987) *Further Voices in Vergil's Aeneid*. Oxford

(1994) 'Vergil's *Aeneid*: subversion by intertextuality', *G&R* 41: 187–204

Mackail, J. W. (1912) 'Virgil's use of the word *ingens*', *CR* 26: 251–5

Malamud, M. A. (1995) 'Happy birthday, dead Lucan: (p)raising the dead in *Silvae* 2.7', *Ramus* 24: 1–30

Maltby, R. (1991) *A Lexicon of Ancient Latin Etymologies*. Leeds

Mariotti, S. (1955) *Il Bellum Poenicum e l'arte di Nevio*. Rome

(1986) *Livio Andronico e la traduzione artistica*. 2nd ed. Urbino

Martindale, C. (1986) *John Milton and the Transformation of Ancient Epic*. London

(1993) *Redeeming the Text: Latin Poetry and the Hermeneutics of Reception*. Cambridge

Masters, J. M. (1992) *Poetry and Civil War in Lucan's Bellum Civile*. Cambridge

Mayer, R. (1982) 'Neronian classicism', *AJP* 103: 305–18

McKeown, J. C. (1987–) *Ovid: Amores*. I: Text and Prolegomena. Liverpool. II: A Commentary on Book One. Leeds

Miller, J. F. (1983) 'Ennius and the elegists', *ICS* 8: 277–95

(1993) 'Ovidian allusion and the vocabulary of memory', *MD* 30: 153–64

Moles, J. L. (1983) 'Virgil, Pompey, and the *Histories* of Asinius Pollio', *CW* 76: 287–8

Morgan, K. (1977) *Ovid's Art of Imitation: Propertius in the Amores*. Leiden

Morris, S. P. (1992) *Daidalos and the Origins of Greek Art*. Princeton

Myers, K. S. (1990) 'Ovid's *tecta ars*: *Amores* 2.6, "programmatics and the parrot"', *EMC* n.s.9: 367–74

(1994) *Ovid's Causes: Cosmogony and Aetiology in the Metamorphoses*. Ann Arbor

Mynors, R. A. B. (1990) *Virgil: Georgics*. Oxford

Narducci, E. (1973) 'Il tronco di Pompeo', *Maia* 25: 317–25

(1979) *La provvidenza crudele: Lucano e la distruzione dei miti augustei*. Pisa

Nicoll, W. S. M. (1980) 'Cupid, Apollo, and Daphne (Ovid, *Met.* 1.452ff.)', *CQ* 30: 174–82

Nisbet, R. G. M. and Hubbard, M. (1978) *A Commentary on Horace, Odes Book II*. Oxford

O'Hara, J. J. (1996) *True Names: Vergil and the Alexandrian Tradition of Etymological Wordplay*. Ann Arbor

O'Higgins, D. (1988) 'Lucan as *vates*', *CA* 7: 208–26

Pasquali, G. (1951) 'Arte allusiva', in *Stravaganze quarte e supreme*. Venice, 11–20

Pelling, C. (1989) 'Plutarch: Roman heroes and Greek culture', in M. Griffin and J. Barnes (eds.), *Philosophia Togata*. Oxford, 199–232

Pernot, L. (1986) 'Lieu et lieu commun dans la rhétorique antique', *BAGB*: 253–84

Pucci, P. (1982) 'The proem of the *Odyssey*', *Arethusa* 15: 39–62

Quint, D. (1989) 'Repetition and ideology in the *Aeneid*', *MD* 23: 9–54 ✕

Rawson, E. (1989) 'Roman rulers and the philosophic adviser', in M. Griffin and J. Barnes (eds.), *Philosophia Togata*. Oxford, 233–57

Richlin, A. (1992) *The Gardens of Priapus: Sexuality and Aggression in Roman Humor*, rev. ed. Oxford

Ricks, C. (1976) 'Allusion: the poet as heir', in R. F. Brissenden and J. C. Eade (eds.), ✕ *Studies in the Eighteenth Century*, III. Toronto, 209–40

Rosati, G. (1983) *Narciso e Pigmalione: Illusione e spettacolo nelle Metamorfosi di Ovidio*. Florence

(1994a) 'Momenti e forme della fortuna antica di Ovidio: l'Achilleide di Stazio', in M. Picone and B. Zimmermann (eds.), *Ovidius redivivus*. Stuttgart, 43–62

(1994b) *Stazio: Achilleide*. Milan

Rosenmeyer, P. A. (1991) 'Simonides' Danae fragment reconsidered', *Arethusa* 24: 5–29

Ross, D. O. (1969) *Style and Tradition in Catullus*. Cambridge, MA

(1975) *Backgrounds to Augustan Poetry: Gallus, Elegy and Rome*. Cambridge

(1987) *Virgil's Elements: Physics and Poetry in the Georgics*. Princeton

Rudd, N. (1989) *Horace: Epistles Book II and Epistle to the Pisones ('Ars Poetica')*. Cambridge

Russell, D. A. (1979) '*De imitatione*' in West and Woodman (1979), 1–16

Shawcross, J. T. (1991) *Intentionality and the New Traditionalism*. University Park, PA

Silk, M. S. (1974) *Interaction in Poetic Imagery*. Cambridge

Skutsch, O. (1985) *The Annals of Quintus Ennius*. Oxford

Smith, R. A. (1990) 'Ov. *Met.* 10.475: an instance of "meta-allusion"', *Gymnasium* 97: 458–60

Solodow, J. B. (1988) *The World of Ovid's Metamorphoses*. Chapel Hill

Stewart, A. F. (1990) *Greek Sculpture*. New Haven

Suerbaum, W. (1968) *Untersuchungen zur Selbstdarstellung älterer römischer Dichter, Livius Andronicus, Naevius, Ennius*. Hildesheim

Tanner, T. (1993) Review of I. Armstrong, *Victorian Poetry*, *Times Literary Supplement* July 2 1993, 12

Thomas, R. F. (1982) 'Catullus and the polemics of poetic reference (64.1–18)', *AJP* 103: 144–64

(1986) 'Virgil's *Georgics* and the art of reference', *HSCP* 90: 171–98

(1988a) *Virgil: Georgics*. Cambridge

(1988b) 'Tree violation and ambivalence in Virgil', *TAPA* 118: 261–73

(1993) Review of N. Horsfall, *Virgilio: L'epopea in alambicco*, *Vergilius* 39: 76–80

Tissol, G. (1993) 'Ovid's little *Aeneid* and the thematic integrity of the *Metamorphoses*', *Helios* 20: 69–79

Verducci, F. (1985) *Ovid's Toyshop of the Heart*. Princeton

Vessey, D. W. T. (1986) '*Pierius menti calor incidit*: Statius' epic style', *ANRW* II. 32.5, 2965–3019

Waszink, J. H. (1979) '*Camena*', in *Opuscula Selecta*. Leiden, 89–98

Weinreich, O. (1926) *Die Distichen des Catull*. Tübingen

West, D. A. and Woodman, A. J. (eds.) (1979) *Creative Imitation and Latin Literature*. Cambridge

White, P. (1987) 'Horace, *Epistles* 2.1.50–54', *TAPA* 117: 227–34

Wigodsky, M. (1972) *Vergil and Early Latin Poetry*. Wiesbaden

Williams, G. (1968) *Tradition and Originality in Roman Poetry*. Oxford

(1978) *Change and Decline: Roman Literature in the Early Empire*. Berkeley

Williams, G. D. (1992) 'Representations of the book-roll in Latin poetry: Ovid, *Tr.* 1.1.3–14 and related texts', *Mnemosyne* 45: 178–89

Williams, R. D. (1973) *The Aeneid of Virgil: Books 7–12*. London

Williams, R. G. (1993) 'I shall be spoken: textual boundaries, authors, and intent', in G. Bornstein and R. G. Williams (eds.), *Palimpsest*. Ann Arbor, 45–66

Wills, J. (1987) '*Scyphus* – a Homeric hapax in Virgil', *AJP* 108: 455–7

(1996) *Repetition in Latin Poetry: Figures of Allusion*. Oxford

Winterbottom, M. (1974) *The Elder Seneca*. 2 vols. Cambridge, MA

Wiseman, T. P. (1974) *Cinna the Poet and other Roman Essays*. Leicester

Worton, M. and Still, J. (eds.) (1990) *Intertextuality: Theories and Practices*. Manchester

Zanker, P. (1988) *The Power of Images in the Age of Augustus*, trans. A. Shapiro. Ann Arbor

Zetzel, J. E. G. (1972) 'Cicero and the Scipionic Circle', *HSCP* 76: 173–9

(1983) 'Catullus, Ennius, and the poetics of allusion', *ICS* 8: 251–66

General index

Index of passages discussed